From me to you

Elyse Knowles
xo

MURDOCH BOOKS

SYDNEY · LONDON

EK

From me
to you
xo

To the beautiful individuals who have followed and supported my career from the beginning. I wish you all the best in your own adventures as you meet your dreams and discover your true potential.

Cherishing the still and simple moments of a day.

Joshy gives me support & encouragement. He's my rock.

It's funny to think that so many people around Australia are beginning to know my name, my face and my laugh so well! It's a little bit surreal, really. I've been working in the modelling industry for about sixteen years, but the last two years especially have been a crazy rollercoaster. I've had both career highlights and moments where I've come face-to-face with some of my biggest challenges.

I am now in a place in my life where I feel calm, focused, grateful, happy, proud and settled. A lot of hard work and commitment have gone into getting myself here – many ups and downs and all the rest. While I'm pretty stoked to be in such a positive place, there is one thing I understand very, very well about myself. As that calm and settled feeling spreads, I know that it's time to take on an adventure and set new goals – even bigger ones.

I was absolutely over the moon when I was approached to write a book, and I jumped into the project with both feet. This is the approach I always take when it comes to life's unique and exciting opportunities. It's important to appreciate these moments and cherish the experiences.

When I was growing up, I wished for a 'directory' that told me the ins and outs of life and all it had to offer. I never found anything that came close to this, so I decided to use this opportunity to write the book I wish I had. From health and wellness to fashion, beauty, business and home renovating, *From Me to You* shares my experiences, what I've learned and how I've felt at different points in my life and career so far. It's a personal look at the cut-throat modelling industry and my day-to-day life.

My intention is to share the various things I've come to realise over the years and to remind you how much beauty there is to living and learning at your own pace, in your own style. If just one person takes something positive from this book, I'll consider my goal accomplished.

I love helping people grow into stronger individuals who genuinely know their worth. Hard work and big commitments can lead to the most extraordinary outcomes, so get – and stay – involved in life. Sure, hurdles will appear along the way, but it's true what they say: what doesn't kill you will only make you stronger.

Right now, my career is on an upswing and I'm doing things I never thought I'd be able to. While I feel very lucky, nothing has ever just landed in my lap. I've worked incredibly hard for years to build my career. It comes down to commitment and pure resilience.

I'm honoured to share my notes, stories and experiences and to invite you into my world. Thank you for sticking with me all these years. It means the world and more.

x Elyse

CHAPTER ONE

My Story

I t's a beautiful thing to realise there are people out there who admire little bits about you: the way you do things, the attitude you choose to adopt and the decisions you make – even though they've never met you! My new challenge is to dig deep and invite you to get to know the real me: the true-blue Elyse Knowles.

From Me to You is both a chance for me to savour this moment in time and (hopefully) to give you a well-rounded picture of me and where I've come from. Remember that almost an entire quarter of a century took place before you heard my name. I'm taking you back to the start – right back to 1992. Buckle up!

Where it all began

I was born on September 30, 1992 in Boronia, Victoria, which is about 40 minutes from the centre of Melbourne. When I was nine months old, my mum and dad, Kim and Stuart, purchased their dream home in Eltham, where they moved to raise us kids. Eltham is a beautiful, leafy-green suburb just north of Melbourne. It's full of winding roads and fresh air. Chirping birds control the neighbourhood playlist instead of Melbourne's signature trams and constant city hustle. My parents felt Eltham was a place where kids could ride bikes, kick a footy in the street and dance around a backyard sprinkler while the smell of sizzling barbecues oozed into the air. It was the perfect place to raise active kids.

Despite the excitement, buying their dream home was not a decision Mum and Dad made overnight. They planned, saved, sacrificed and worked their butts off to make sure they could make that house with the big 'For Sale' sign their own home. And they did it. I think hearing this story over the years may explain where my love of the property market stemmed from.

Right from the beginning, Dad knew that this home would be where we'd all grow up. He could see our lives maturing from nappies to adulthood within these four walls. For years, he put his game face on and worked fiercely to make the monthly mortgage repayments. Mum stayed home to raise three kids, a job no easier. She had two *normal* kids and one called 'the Hell Child'. You guessed it: I was 'the Hell Child'. It was a name I was given not long after Mum had me because I never stopped crying and flat-out refused to let anyone who wasn't Mum hold me. If the roles had been reversed, I would've given me to the neighbours in a heartbeat! Mum was one patient woman. She bit her lip and eventually transformed my tears to smiles.

Growing up in that house was nothing but a joy — a chaotic, loud, circus-like joy, but a joy nonetheless. To this day, it is still our family home. Mum and Dad paid it off a few years back, so they can now relax a little without a mortgage looming over their heads. On second thought, the word 'relax' might be too strong. Yes, Dad got his dream watching his three kids grow up under one roof, but he probably didn't anticipate the additional two boyfriends, one girlfriend and two dogs that he'd inherit over the years. Sorry, Dad.

Childhood days

Within our immediate family, I'm the eldest of three. My younger brother, Brayden, is 23 (two years younger than me) and my little sister, Tahlea, is 21. None of us kids were given a middle name. After the accomplishment of having each baby, Mum found it hard enough coming up with the energy to assign one name per baby, let alone two! Her list of names was already almost used up by the time Tahlea was born. She went nameless for six whole days.

After naming us, the real challenge began: feeding us. Luckily for Mum, we were all easy tummies to fill. As long as there was

Snippets of a very happy childhood

a pot of plain pasta topped with sprinkles of parmesan cheese, no tears or tantrums erupted at the dinner table. No joke, that is all we ever wanted. It's probably not the most nutritious meal, but for three very active, hungry kids, it did the trick. I've popped the method here. Please feel free to take this recipe for your own friends and families!

A-grade recipe here, guys! $\longrightarrow$

1. Boil water.
2. Cook pasta.
3. Pop into a bowl.
4. Sprinkle over parmesan or any cheese of your choice.

While that isn't a terribly good example, Mum was (and still is) outrageously creative. She used to teach a ceramics class in the downstairs family room four times a week, with 20 people in each class. I would sit on the stairs and watch in awe. Anything remotely artistic caught my eye in a heartbeat.

During class, Mum's students would comment on how cute and well behaved I was. I'd perch silently on the stairs and watch the class unfold while dressed in the little nighties Mum had sewn me with their matching shoes. Fashion was a keen interest of Mum's. She studied it before Brayden, Tahlea and I came along and continued to make time for it. She'd become a fantastic seamstress.

Mum's love of fashion and sewing was a great thing — most of the time. It was great until she made the three of us wear matching outfits. We looked like *The Brady Bunch*. It was horrifying. No matter how hard we fought those outfits, she won every single time.

As I grew a little bigger, ceramics night became a favourite of mine for a different reason: it was one of the rare times Mum was completely off duty. In other words, it provided the perfect opportunity to bash Brayden up! There was no one around to protect the baby boy since Dad would just laugh, so I was in the perfect position to pounce. I had really long legs and — during my earlier years — was a lot bigger than Brayden, so I had a huge advantage. Most of the time I wanted to prove that despite being a girl, I was strong, too. I'd sit on Brayden's head, giggling at my poor prey.

Dad was the one who encouraged our love of the outdoors and the beauty of staying active. Right from our early years, he taught us how to ride the family motorbike (the Pee Wee 50, which Dad later upgraded for a CRF100 Honda), how to swim and how to play water sports. He figured the younger we were, the less fear we would have. He'd lovingly throw us into the deep end and watch as we became stronger and more confident.

The best thing about motorbikes and water sports was that it took us out of the city and into the bush. Before I'd even turned two years old, Dad had bought the family a speedboat. From then on, and right up to today, we started going up to the river with our collection of toys: tents, swags, eskies, tarps, outdoor showers, barbecues, sleeping bags and tucker. If you want to survive a camping trip with the Knowles family, you can't be precious. We camp the proper way, like troopers.

Our speedboat was great for water skiing, wake surfing, wake boarding, bare footing and pretty much anything else that involves water. Many of you will have seen photos of the boat by now on my Instagram. I started to kneeboard from the time I was four years old. I took to it quite naturally, though there was one big fall that royally spooked me. After a fast turn I fell off the side of the board and, frozen with fear, forgot to let go of the handle. I held on for so long underwater, I swear the fish were staring back at me thinking, 'What is this girl doing under here?' Dad quickly dove into the water and scooped me up, but it was a good year before I was brave enough to get behind the boat and back on that board. Now it's virtually impossible to get me off.

I cherish these annual family trips to the river. We all do. We take friends up with us and hang out for weeks. It's so nice to be out of the city, living amongst nature where the hum of traffic is drowned out by rustling trees, boat motors, laughter and roaring camp fires. As I get older and my career becomes more serious, getting out amongst nature is the best way to switch off and check out for a little while. It does my psyche wonders.

Finding my way

I wasn't the brightest cookie when it came time for school. In third grade, I started receiving tutoring in nearly all of my subjects. My tutor would come to our house after school and I would sit there in agony, trying to understand the confusing world of maths and

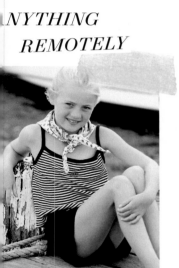

ANYTHING
REMOTELY

ARTISTIC
*CAUGHT
MY EYE
in a*
HEARTBEAT.

This photo represents my perfect holiday: fresh air,
family and peace.

The Knowles kids welcomed any kind of outdoorsy activity,
playing (or fighting!) until the sun went down.

science. To make matters worse, I was also in Reading Recovery, a side class created to help kids improve their reading skills. I had to take double the required classes.

There I was, cooped up in a classroom or at home after school with a tutor (who I am, of course, very grateful to), when I just wanted to be outside running around and kicking a footy with my friends. I had to suck it up and stick it out for Three. Whole. Years. It felt like the universe was giving me the raw end of the stick.

By the time I graduated primary school and entered high school, I needed slightly less academic assistance. I continued with my maths tutor and took an extra English class (which the kids at school called 'special English') to make sure I stayed on track. There's no point fighting these things. You have to admit your weaknesses and do your best to improve. Despite a few hiccups in some areas, I flourished in others.

YOU HAVE TO ADMIT YOUR WEAKNESSES AND DO YOUR BEST TO IMPROVE.

Any troubles or negative energy I felt toward maths, English and science, I soon learnt to convert into a flow of boundless creative energy. I started to dominate in art, fashion, sport, cooking, outdoor ed and drama. One year I played the main role in our school play. I felt like I'd found my calling in the world of art, sports and entertainment.

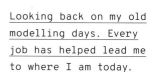

Looking back on my old modelling days. Every job has helped lead me to where I am today.

Getting into modelling

I began modelling when I was only 10 years old. My agency at the time was a specialised agency for children and they introduced me to some of my earliest clients, including family brands such as Target.

I remember my first few years in the industry as if they were yesterday. Waking up on the days when a modelling job was

Every time this fear crept in, I reminded myself why I was there and how amazing the opportunity was.

booked was the best. I loved being in front of the camera and being surrounded by a creative team full of passion. I remember bursting through the studio doors with a beaming smile on my face, oozing excitement every time.

It wasn't always like that. In the early days, when I was required to be in front of the camera I felt super shy. Sometimes I was so nervous I'd get up there and totally freeze. Every time this fear crept in, I reminded myself why I was there and how amazing the opportunity was. It was up to me to relax and give it my best shot. After getting used to the photographers, the lighting, and so on, my confidence grew. With every shoot, I came out of my shell more and more. Finally, it all kicked in and I started to feel that this was exactly where I was meant to be.

When you're a little kid, modelling is all cute and sweet. You look similar to the other kids on set; your skin is smooth and your hair is always clean and shiny. As you get older, especially as a girl, everything changes. It's awkward, uncomfortable and a bit weird. You grow up and out, you don't smell as rosy as you used to and your mood goes up and down like a yo-yo. In sixth grade, when I was 12, I started to get boobs! At 14 I was inches taller than my peers, while around the same time my skin decided to exchange smoothness for bumps.

It was at this point that Mum and I decided it was time for me to move on from the children's agency. World of boobs, hips and lanky legs, here I come.

By the time I was 15 and halfway through high school, my modelling career had developed a lot and I had the opportunity to live and work in Hong Kong for four months. The thought of moving to a foreign city where the locals don't really speak your language, there are no friends or family to lean on and you have to balance your education and job at the same time was scary.

Before jetting off to Hong Kong, I found myself in the midst of shifting from modelling as a 'girl' to modelling as a 'woman'. It was an intense transition. All of a sudden I was surrounded by a flock of tall, skinny models. They were all so intimidating and looked hungry enough to eat me! I set aside my fears and replaced them with a brave face. I was going to do what needed to be done to fit in, which apparently meant moving to a foreign city. Eek.

**BE YOU,
AND BE YOU
ALWAYS!**

A bump in the road

There I was, bags packed, ready for my modelling adventure in Hong Kong. I was told it would 'make my career'. In hindsight, I wish I'd stayed home. Luckily for me, Mum came along for the first month to help me settle in. I was only 15, after all, and needed help to find my bearings. We're talking about the same girl who was taking double English. Taking on Cantonese was going to be a slight challenge, to say the least.

Mum and I shared an apartment with two lovely girls who instantly took me under their wings. We slowly got to know each other, explored our local suburb and went out for dinner at night. The restaurants always seemed to erupt into parties toward the end of the night, but the three of us would ignore the chaos and walk happily back to our apartment. We were there to work, not to party — especially with strangers.

One night on Halloween, after Mum had returned home to Melbourne, the three of us went out for our usual dinner. Since it was Halloween, my two housemates decided it would be fun to stay out a little later than usual. Not wanting to cause a fuss or seem difficult, I agreed.

It wasn't long before alcohol filled the room and strange, sleazy men rolled into the restaurant, giving us looks. A group of guys eventually ushered us over to sit with them and insisted we have a drink. Scared out of my brains, I had a drink. After just one, I felt weird and out of sorts. By this point the other girls were too drunk to notice, so I felt scared and alone. I decided to leave.

In situations like these, models — and young women in general — have to be proactive and headstrong. If you're sitting with someone who makes you uncomfortable, remove yourself and head home or into a safe environment. Ask a friend to come with you or, at the very least, tell your friends that you've decided to leave so they know where you are. Call a parent or a trusted friend and arrange a lift home. Depending on where you are in the world, Ubers and taxis may be safe alternatives, but do research before arriving in a foreign city. I can't stress this point enough. A little research ahead of time is crucial in terms of your safety.

My strong advice: if you decide to leave a situation, always get your girlfriend or group of girlfriends to come with you. They might

Mum & me
Hong Kong, 2008

be annoyed for an hour or so, but they'll get over it. Your safety is worth far more than a silly tiff with your mate. And, of course, never, ever leave a friend completely by herself. The world can be a dangerous place and, sadly, young women can fall prey to people with no hearts and no souls. Even if they just want to buy you a quick drink, say no and walk away. If you feel even the slightest bit uncomfortable, something is not right. Trust your gut 100 percent and head home.

On this particular night out in Hong Kong, I couldn't call or text anyone as it was before we all had iPhones. There were no cabs in sight and everyone outside on the street was off their head after a big night of drinking. There was only one option: I sprinted home! For 20 minutes it was a complete blur. I ran so fast I can barely remember the path I took. I remember being terrified of someone jumping out from around a dark corner and mugging me or worse. I don't think I've ever run so hard or so fast.

When I got home and closed the door behind me, relief rushed through my bones. It was obvious that my drink had been spiked with god-knows-what, leaving me all woozy. I showered and went to bed. No more nights out. That was the scariest night I had growing up and from that day on, I promised myself that I would speak up whenever I felt uncomfortable and would trust my gut and nothing else.

For the next three months, I stayed in Hong Kong, desperate to make the trip worth it and excel at my modelling career. I put up with what I had to and got through each day, praying for work. And then the Global Financial Crisis hit. Great.

The GFC turned the already chaotic buzz of this bustling city into complete mayhem. People lined up for ages outside banks, ready to withdraw every dollar they had. Everyone was saving their pennies and spending only on essentials, like food. This of course meant that no one, not even the big fashion businesses, was booking models to promote new clothes and accessories. There was no one around to buy them. The city just sort of shut down. It was a depressing place to be.

I was stuck. Go back to Melbourne or stick it out here? I had no idea what to do or who I should listen to. My agency in Melbourne advised me to ride it out. I followed their advice, but moved to another city, Guangzhou, which was known for its mass production so I would be more likely to book work there. This couldn't have been further from the truth. There was no modelling work in Guangzhou either.

My experience in this new city was even worse. Even writing about it gives me the shudders. I moved into the agency's house with nine other models from all over the world. Most of them didn't speak English, so communication was hard. I couldn't even go out for a walk because I was told it was too dangerous. To add to this already disastrous experience, I became so ill from the polluted air that I was instructed to stay in bed for a week. I now appreciate why people in pockets of Asia wear masks over their mouths. The pollution is vile. We are so spoilt by the clean air in Australia.

The conditions were so bad that sewage began to flow out of the shower drain. I would Skype Mum, Dad and my then-boyfriend in tears, wanting to come home. I wished I'd never listened to my agency and had booked a flight straight out of there. Being that unhappy was harming my health and my state of mind. I became angrier every day, knowing that this was just about money for my agency and was in complete disregard for my wellbeing.

My fourth month abroad finally came to a close and my contract was up, so I went home. Landing in Melbourne felt like a dream. I was desperate to get off the plane into the sunshine and fresh air and back home to my family. I was so excited to get home that I completely forgot to collect my bag at the airport in Melbourne! I sprinted off the plane and into the arms of my family.

After any negative experience, I find it important to find something good: a silver lining. In this case I found three things — a newfound appreciation for my family and home, a thicker skin and a sharper mind. I swore I'd never again do what people told me to without doing my own thorough research.

AFTER ANY NEGATIVE EXPERIENCE, I FIND IT IMPORTANT TO FIND SOMETHING GOOD — A SILVER LINING.

A fresh start

After arriving back in Australia, I returned to school and quickly found a new agency. If you don't have a solid relationship with your agent in this industry, it's important to move on.

My teachers kindly welcomed me back. I noticed, however, that they disliked it when I needed to leave class early for a modelling job. Now I understand why, but at the time I didn't see what the problem was, since I always completed my homework and handed it in on time. Truth be told, Elyse Knowles was a Little Miss Goody-Two-Shoes. Yep, I was one of them! But despite that, I didn't get any special favours from the teachers.

It wasn't long before Mum was called into the principal's office and asked to explain why modelling was so important to me and why I couldn't give it up. Mum successfully convinced the principal that I was smart enough, committed enough and determined enough to do both modelling and school. And I did! I ended up graduating high school with a final score of 73 in my exams — not too shabby, if you ask me. And now all these years later, I'm writing a book. Who would have thought?

I was however lucky to have many accepting teachers and peers throughout my time at school — as well as a family who backs me without hesitation. I certainly wouldn't be here without them. It was Mum's support in particular that meant I could physically rock up to castings and jobs over the years. During my time at school, Mum drove me everywhere. I hate to think of how many kilometres we clocked up, let alone how many litres of fuel were guzzled.

To this day, Mum loves coming to shoots with me to watch or lend a hand. She's always reminded me to give everything my all and to never, ever give up, even if I'm having a bad day. She's taught me to treat everyone on set like they were the director — to be kind, courteous and polite. And she was right: trust me when I say that simple manners will get you very far in this business.

It was amazing when my modelling career started to take off, but it didn't happen overnight. It took years before I landed my first real job. After each casting, I remember coming home and praying that I'd get the job. I'd been to well over 150 castings before a client finally booked me for a campaign. The day it happened, I bounced with excitement. I had booked a Jay Jays campaign!

The excitement was like nothing else. When the campaign came out, my photos were there in the shops, hung in store windows for everyone on the street to see. There was even a giant poster with my face on it hung on the freeway! I knew that I had to make this feeling last. It was time to work even harder.

When you set your eye on a goal, you need to do research. Learn everything you can about how things work, who people are, what kinds of people you are inspired by and whose career path you'd love to follow. For me, that last one was easy. Growing up, my inspiration was Miranda Kerr. She was beautiful, humble and successful. I remember seeing her on the cover of *Dolly* magazine in April 1997, right after she'd won their modelling competition. I started to read about her and where she came from. I set up a file on my computer and saved images from her photo shoots so I could learn about her poses, shapes and angles. I wanted to learn from the very best — and she was it. I discovered that she was known for being a hard worker and a perfectionist. When she was on a shoot, she always asked for feedback on things she could improve upon. This was exactly the type of model I wanted to be: dedicated, professional and focused.

Finding strength in independence

After the Jay Jays campaign, the number of jobs I booked became more consistent. I was working hard and I'd started to earn a little more money, too. It felt a bit strange to be earning money so young when there was not a lot to spend it on. This is when Dad taught me about the power of saving. He said that by saving my income, I'd be able to invest in things that would mean a lot more to me than movies, clothes and magazines.

The day my modelling savings had been enough to buy myself a Baby Born was a big day, but the day my savings were enough to buy a car was an even bigger day! Over the years, I started to love the feeling of saving and developing financial independence. It's liberating and empowering to work hard enough that you can start to build your dream life, brick by brick.

During my schooling days, I remained dedicated, professional and focused. I have never been a big party girl. Even after I

Build your dream life, brick by brick.

Where it all began! This Jay Jays campaign was a really big moment for me.

graduated high school and everyone started hitting the club scene, I didn't see the need to waste my money on drinks and entry fees. I had bigger things in mind. I wanted to travel the world and save for a house.

With hard work, savings, work opportunities and supportive relationships, I've managed to get my travel and property goals comfortably underway. And whilst I continue to chip away at them, I am also constantly adding more things to the bucket list: places to go, clients to work with, new challenges to have a crack at. Having things to aim for is a wonderful way to live and grow.

Fortunately, this driven mindset and way of living fits seamlessly with the people I love the most. Since my story began, two new characters have been thrown into the mix: Josh, my amazing partner, and our dog Isla (who now rules our house and gets away with absolutely everything!). Josh and Isla have made my life feel even more special. Day after day, they add nothing but happiness, love and positivity.

And then, of course, there is my family: four of the best people on the planet. Mum and Dad keep me strong and grounded, and like all good siblings, Brayden and Tahlea tell me to harden up on the bad days and celebrate with me on good days.

So, there you have it folks! The story of Elyse before you met her in a catalogue, on social media or on *The Block*. I'm so excited to be writing this book and sharing with you my stories, observations, ideas and little bits of advice. I am not an expert in any field but my own, so the following chapters are here for you to do what you will with. I hope there's a little something in here for every one of you.

THE KNOWLES FAMILY

Meet my mum, Kim

MY ROCK

So much of my life and career is thanks to my family. They back me every single day and never leave my side. Since I mention them so much throughout the book, I thought you might like to hear their take on things! I asked my friend Tori Bowman to sit down with Mum, Dad, Tahlea, Brayden and Josh to pick their brains. They were each asked a series of questions and you'll find their answers throughout the book. Who knows what they all had to say? Fingers crossed they were kind! First up is Mum.

It's obvious how much Elyse adores her mum! You've been a pivotal part of her career to date and a best friend who has always had her back. When was the moment you realised how headstrong and determined Elyse really was?
Elyse was determined to make her modelling career work from a very young age. As a teenager she had to balance her VCE (Victorian Certificate of Education) and a part-time café job, while also trying to establish and grow her modelling career.

I would pick Elyse up during school hours to get to a casting on time. Elyse would jump in, get dressed in the car, do her make-up on the freeway and then stand in a queue with 50 other girls waiting for their five-minute casting. When Elyse was done, I'd whizz her back to school to make sure she could attend the final few hours of class time. If we didn't make it back, the school coordinator could get pretty cranky!

Elyse had knock back after knock back, but nothing stopped her. I remember when one of Elyse's agents took photos of her at 16. After the shots were taken, the agent sat Elyse down and told her that she had a lazy eye. It broke my heart to watch Elyse cry that night, so upset by that comment. I asked her if she wanted to find something else to pour her passion into, but from that moment on Elyse's determination grew stronger! Nothing was getting in her way.

To you, personally, what is it about Elyse that makes her who she is?
She is special in her own way. Elyse is very strong minded and has always been determined to help people in need. Elyse is also grounded and easygoing, always saying things to me such as, 'It is what it is Mum,' 'Be the person you are,' and 'Don't worry about what other people think!' She accepts that bad days occur and there are things in life that are simply out of our control, but Elyse chooses to move onwards and upwards every time.

Now, be honest: when Elyse and Josh moved back home after *The Block* for a few months, what were her worst habits?
Elyse seems to love leaving her teapot out somewhere special for me to find and wash up. And you are not allowed to wash the mug that Elyse is using. This is a flat-out no-no. Elyse uses the same mug all day long. She continuously refills it with hot water. No one is to go near the mug.

And if she comes home after a long day of work to find no one has walked the dogs, watch out, folks! She will crack it.

Can you summarise Elyse in a collection of words?
Genuine, ambitious, thoughtful, loving, outgoing, adventurous, friendly, sociable, approachable, extroverted, charitable and courageous.

CHAPTER
TWO

From Me
to You

After working in the modelling industry for so long, I understand all too well the risk of comparing myself to others. Trust me. During my first few years of modelling I was always concerned about my height, my hips, my hair. Would I ever be as tall as her, as lean as her, as flawless as her, as *good* as her?

Looking back, these thoughts now seem so odd because apart from their heights and hip sizes, I didn't know anything about those girls – their personalities, their backgrounds, their aspirations. I was idolising total strangers for the most superficial reasons, which is not healthy. I want to be inspired by people because of their voices, their opinions, their lifestyles and their hearts, not because of the size and shape of their limbs. That's a little ridiculous, wouldn't you agree?

Delete the negative

Social media certainly hasn't made it easy for our generation in terms of body image and self-confidence. I am the first to admit that scrolling through photos of 'perfect people' with 'perfect lives' can be intimidating. Some of you might look at my feed and think I'm perfect. But remember, the majority of us use social media to share the moments we want to remember. We pop them up to tag and include our friends and family or to mark a positive occasion.

There are many moments in the life of Elyse Knowles that I wouldn't punish your eyes with! When it's 11 pm at night and I'm exhausted and grumpy, I still haven't packed for a flight that leaves super early the next morning and Isla is looking up at me with her sweet little eyes saying, 'Mummy, I miss you. Don't leave me again.' I spare you these details. Or when I'm running around getting ready for a home inspection — cleaning the oven, mopping the floors, picking up dog poo and begging Josh to put his shoes on and stop mowing the lawn (which we don't have to worry about anymore — woo!) I can guarantee that you have far better things to do than to watch this.

Regardless of what I see and post on social media, I've made a conscious effort to focus more on the inner beauty of the women I follow. I want to think less about a woman's figure and learn more about her heart, soul and what drives her. If you find yourself on Instagram looking at accounts that don't inspire you, don't motivate you or don't make you feel positive in some way, here's a little tip: click 'unfollow', pronto.

WHEN IT COMES TO SOCIAL MEDIA, THE POWER IS IN YOUR HANDS!

We all have the power of choice when it comes to social media. Choose to use it for good. If you find that it is intimidating you at any point, something is not right, so make a change. When it comes to social media, the power is in your hands.

Trust me when I say that you will not miss out on anything if you have the guts to unfollow a few accounts here and there. You'll actually gain so much. You'll gain relief, happiness, confidence, time and energy. All from one click. Go on, girls! Delete the negative in your life.

You are good enough

Writing this book is a beautiful opportunity for me to speak to girls and women who, like I did, worry about never being quite good enough. I'm treating this chapter as a mini 'powwow', to remind you that despite what you might think or feel about yourself in this moment, you are incredible. You are beautiful, unique and amazing just the way you are. That area of your body you are never at peace with? The haircut you hate? The eyebrows you desperately want fixed? None of that affects the brilliance you're capable of bringing into the world — unless you let it. Be courageous and try not to get hung up on these superficial things. If you embrace yourself and back your mind and body to the full extent, confidence will follow.

In my experience, confidence comes with time. Time and self-acceptance. I'm going to give you a challenge. Think about something you love about yourself. What is something you truly think is beautiful? Something that makes you feel lucky. Now write it down on a piece of paper. (You don't have to show anyone.) Write one thing down every day for a week. For seven days in a row, I challenge you to find a moment during your busy day to bring yourself some confidence and joy.

The point of this little challenge is to remind you that we can't always rely on others to present us with compliments or pats on the back. Confidence has to come from within.

Confidence is not about arrogance; it's about strength of character. In many ways, it's a form of kindness. You're allowed to be kind to yourself and to befriend your own body. In fact, that's the goal! Don't you find that the people you consider to be the world's most beautiful are those who are comfortable in their own skin? They ooze self-assurance. This is what makes them beautiful: their happiness. They're content, humble and satisfied with who they are. This is what I personally work toward every day.

If you do want to tone up, improve your fitness, better your diet or increase your energy level, by all means do so. It's normal to want to feel your best. Create a plan, stick to it and make it happen. Don't let the task ahead make it all seem too hard. Don't punish your mind with negative thoughts of dread and doubt before you give yourself the chance to smash your goal. But activate your

Confidence has to come from within.

Out of so many photos, I love the oldies the most.

When you are relaxed in your own skin, the confidence
will shine from within.

goal sooner rather than later. There is no time like the present. Choose to be a do-er. I know you can do it. I know you'll blitz it!

Being kind to yourself is so important. Sometimes I take a few days off working out if I'm exhausted or if I'm travelling a lot. When I get back into it, it always takes me a few sessions to regain my strength. It's easy to feel frustrated that my fitness levels have dropped and everything feels harder. It's at this point, however, that I choose not to sulk and instead keep pushing until I get back to where I want to be. After every session, I finish the workout thinking 'Woo! I'm one step closer,' instead of thinking 'Ugh, I'm still not there yet.' A simple change in perspective does wonders. A little bit of kindness goes a long way.

Quit the comparisons

Let's chat about the idea of comparisons. If you haven't already come across it, #QuitTheComparisons is a recent push by women for women. Search the hashtag on Instagram and check it out. The whole thing is designed to remind girls and women to quit looking at *her* and focus on *you*. It's a celebration of all shapes and sizes.

Now, let me ask you something. If you love and believe in this idea and you'd like to see the movement succeed, what are you personally doing, or willing to do, to support it? What part are you going to play to encourage this positive movement among women? It's a tough question.

Here's another test for you. How many of you scroll past a photo on Instagram and think, 'What an awesome cause,' or 'What an inspirational quote. I totally agree,' and then scroll right past it to another photo and think, 'Far out! How do I get my bum to be as toned as hers?' or 'Wow! Her body is out of control.'

I thought so. Don't worry, we are all guilty of this sometimes, myself included.

So, here is my idea. Let's all get behind this movement and encourage ourselves and our friends and family to quit the comparisons. The next time you see an inspirational quote, a meme or a photo on Instagram that makes you feel good, I challenge you to go through your Instagram feed and unfollow at least one account that you know deep down doesn't add value to your self-esteem and your confidence. Go on, I dare ya! I'll be doing it, too.

If it's not on Instagram and you just see something or meet someone who makes you feel good about yourself, pass on the favour. Call or text a friend and make an effort to make them feel great about themselves. It's easy to make someone's day brighter.

Remember that social media is just a tiny little snippet of a very big picture: the big picture being real life. Getting rid of one account here and there is not going to put a dent in your life.

It has sadly become too normal and natural for girls and women to look around and think, 'she's fitter,' 'she's leaner,' 'those boots look so much better on her,' 'why doesn't my skin glow like hers?' or 'how do I get her body?' ... the list goes on. The reality is, we all tend to be our own worst nightmares by forcing ourselves to become fixated on things that, first, are far removed from reality and, second, are far from being important. As women, we need to give ourselves a break. We have bigger things to focus on, right?

See yourself in others

I was reading recently about the idea of seeing yourself in others: seeing beyond yourself. Instead of looking at someone and pointing out what she has and you don't (in other words, what makes her different from you), try to spot the similarities. Look for things in the people you admire that you have in common. I love this idea because it puts a positive spin on things. It helps us realise what we share with those we look up to. It's powerful.

The next time you are admiring someone from afar, you're probably admiring them because you share a common interest — maybe a love of health and wellness or a strong work ethic. Thinking of it this way is far more meaningful than comparing yourself based on what differentiates you.

As Hillary Clinton said, 'Talent is universal, opportunity is not. Particularly for women.' This is such an important idea, so use it to motivate you. You have the ability to be a leader and do great things — we all do if we open our eyes to life's endless paths and possibilities, and if we're brave enough to ask for help and guidance when we need it.

When next you wake up to a bad hair day or your jeans feel a bit tight, try your best to think bigger than that. Life is too short to focus on little insecurities that come and go. Way too short. Try to harness the feeling of gratitude instead.

I understand that most of us will have times where we worry about something to do with our bodies. I get it. It's a part of life and emotions; we are human, after all. But if we are lucky enough to have two legs, two arms, a healthy beating heart and the ability to see and hear the world and those we love, we are lucky. The size of our waists, hips, boobs and bottoms affects nothing at all.

You are amazing just the way you are

If after you've read this chapter you still want to work on something like your fitness or health, go for gold. There are plenty of great tips and tricks in the chapters to come. Just make sure you're doing it for the right reasons. Do it because you have the potential to feel a little better or brighter. Don't do it because she did. And as I said in the beginning, regardless of the change you want to make, you will always be beautiful, unique and amazing the way you are.

My final note in this little 'powpow' is a quick one about social media. When things go online, they can be hard to take offline. It's the pits when you post something and then regret it, but the world has already seen it. Ensure that everything you post is something you're proud of and that is genuinely you. As great as social platforms are for sharing, you're also allowed to keep things to yourself.

Try to harness the feeling of gratitude.

Q&A
MUSES & INSPIRATION

Megan Gale

Megan Gale is one of Australia's top models
as well as an actress, brand ambassador, fashion
designer and philanthropist – in other words,
an Australian wonder woman.

Q. What have you once disliked about yourself that you now love? What changed and led you to appreciate that quality?

A. My lips. A boy at school, who I liked, used to tease me about them as they were bigger and fuller than the average person's and I was super self-conscious about them. I used to press them together to try and thin them out! At 12 years of age, I didn't know any better or have any idea that my full lips would be considered an asset in the industry that I would later be involved in, which, of course, further down the track made me appreciate them as a feature. But I do remember my mum telling me that they were not something to be self-conscious about and she encouraged me to have a lot of self-acceptance from a young age, something I will be forever thankful for.

Q. Is there something about you that might surprise people? Any little superstitions or daily habits?

A. Every night before I drift off to sleep I count ten things that I'm thankful for. They can be important, special things like my kids or my partner or smaller things like getting to go to yoga that day or being out in the sunshine. Often I fall asleep while doing it and it's a lovely peaceful and positive way to fall asleep.

Q. What intimidates you most about the modelling industry? And how do you conquer this?

A. Not much intimidates me about it now, but the unpredictability of it used to unsettle me a lot when I was starting out. Not knowing when your next job is coming, how much you'll be earning for that year, if you could afford your bills, etc. Even once I got to work at a higher level, I still never knew at what point my contract would be renewed, if at all. That's why I encourage young girls to carve out an additional career for themselves beyond modelling and have a back-up plan or something else to move onto that's more secure and reliable.

*'Every night before
I drift off to sleep
I count ten things that
I'm thankful for.'*

–Megan Gale

49

'While it would be tempting
to go back and advise and warn
yourself of certain dangers and
pitfalls, I think everyone's path is
meant to go a certain way including
the good, the bad, the ugly – all of it.
It all shapes us and makes us who we
are and takes us on to the next step
of our individual journey.'

–Megan Gale

Q. If you could sit down with your 16-year-old self, what would you tell her?

A. I've been asked a similar question before and my answer is always the same. While it would be tempting to go back and advise and warn yourself of certain dangers and pitfalls, I think everyone's path is meant to go a certain way including the good, the bad, the ugly — all of it. It all shapes us and makes us who we are and takes us on to the next step of our individual journey. If I were to go back and tweak and change things, I wouldn't get to where I am today, and where I am is where I am meant to be.

Q. Who inspires you? Do you have a mentor?

A. I am inspired by people who have originality, who are driven, who have ambition, confidence and persistence, but who also conduct themselves with integrity and compassion. I've never had a mentor, but I've always sought the advice and guidance from those around me that I trust, be that industry peers or loved ones.

Q. How do you refrain from comparing yourself to others?

A. It's hard not to do that from time to time as it's human nature for all of us to do it on some level. What's important, I think, is to have the self-awareness to catch yourself when you are doing it and acknowledge that it is a waste of your own energy. That energy would be far better spent on striving to improve yourself and your own life, rather than being envious of someone else's.

Q. Model, businesswoman, ambassador, mum: how do you find time to switch off and recharge?

A. I've learnt to do that over time. I used to find it hard to switch off, but my kids are more than enough motivation to do that, as is my health. If I didn't unplug, reset and recharge from time to time, it would result in a complete burnout and then I would be of no use to anyone. I want to be the best that I can be as a mum, a partner to my man, in my work and to my loved ones. The only way I can achieve that fully is to look after myself, and that often requires switching off from the outside world.

Q. In a word, how do you feel about life right now?

A. Content.

CHAPTER THREE

Working Your Way Up

I know what some of you may be thinking. You've seen the name of this chapter and now you're mumbling something along the lines of, 'I know, I know. I've heard it all before when it comes to working hard to achieve my goals.' Am I close? I bet I am. But bear with me – and if you get bored, flip to the next chapter and come back to this a little later.

I wanted to include a chapter of this nature because so many people around my age (meaning, in their twenties) are in such a rush: a rush to do this, do that, try this, try that, go here, go there. Everyone is in a hurry to get to the top, wherever that is. I've been guilty of this, absolutely! The last two years, however, have been a huge eye-opener for me. I've had some amazing moments and have been let down by people who I thought had my back. I've had to make risky decisions involving my career, and emotional decisions involving the selling of my home. I've lived in the public eye via social media and television and I've come out thinking, 'Holy moly! What now? Where to next?'

Life these days and its relentless and unpredictable schedule means that rushing to 'the top' is virtually impossible, because 'the top' seems to shift every day. Is anyone with me on this? I get exhausted trying to figure out how the world works because technology seems to change everything I do and how I do it every two seconds! The minute I get used to my phone or my computer, an updated version is launched and I have to start all over again. This constant state of change makes it tricky to steer our lives and careers in any one particular direction. My career to date has been here, there and everywhere. I look back on some days and think, 'How on earth did I get there?'

Yes, the world and technology changes quickly and constantly. It can make life feel scary because we never know what roadblocks and hurdles to expect and prepare for. But if you can slow down a tiny, little bit and focus on one thing at a time, you'll find your path and be able to stick to the track.

I've made a conscious effort lately to think less about what everyone else is doing and focus more on developing my core values, a positive mindset and a thick skin. If I can nail these things, I'll be able to take on whatever life throws at me.

The next time you hit a hiccup, instead of thinking, 'What am I doing? Where am I going in life?' and rushing forward for the sake of keeping busy — stop, find your bearings and breathe. It will all be okay.

This is exactly what I am doing at the moment. I'm sitting to write this book to reflect on everything to date. It's helping me highlight what I've done and where I want to go next. I hope you find some value within the next few pages, but more than that, I hope to shed light on areas of life that were once grey to me and may be grey to you. Life is about lighting up the path so everyone in your wake can see the beauty ahead.

So here we go: my views on working your way up — not to 'the top', just up. One step at a time toward that dream goal of yours. And remember to slow down a little as you go and enjoy every day. Life is not a race.

Life is a marathon, not a sprint! Take it one step at a time.

One step at a time

One of the best feelings is when I accomplish something I thought was unlikely or, better yet, impossible. It gives me an amazing feeling of invincibility and I feel proud of myself for having the courage to have a crack. It's a boring way to live, always thinking 'I can't,' or 'what if,' or 'I wish'. Less thinking, more doing!

Like most people, I've had moments in my career when I've doubted myself and moments when I've gone into a situation knowing that I'm about to go head-to-head with a tough challenge. But there is no point letting fear distract me or keep me from doing what I want to do in life — absolutely zero point. Nowadays when I feel a sense of fear creeping in, I take a moment to remember that I am where I am for a reason. If I'm walking into a big shoot, I tell myself that I was booked for the job because of who I am, my personality and my look. I was invited to be here in this moment, so there is no reason to feel fearful.

I realised in my first few years in the industry that if I don't give myself that little nudge of reassurance, and instead let my nerves show their ugly face, I become instantly zapped of energy. My confidence dwindles and I end up feeling overwhelmed. It's crazy how quickly one little thought of doubt can spin you out. When this happens, stay calm, take a deep breath and remind yourself how capable you are.

For every hurdle I face, I try to stay focused on the bigger picture. This helps me keep perspective and takes the pressure off. If I can get over one hurdle, I'll be one step closer to the end goal. Life is a marathon, not a sprint! Take it one step at a time.

It's easy to feel as if you have to do everything all at once and tick off a million goals in a short period of time to feel productive or successful. No, no, no! Slow and steady wins the race. Isn't that what all the wise owls out there say? Work on quality over quantity. For example, if I'm having a quiet period at work, rushing to book four or five jobs I don't really want just for the sake of feeling busy is not going to help me in the long run. I'm better off staying positive and being patient.

My goals and my 'big-picture plan' change every so often as I get older. I meet new people and discover new things, causing the goal posts to move around. Despite the changes, having goals constantly in my mind keeps me motivated to work hard every day.

I was 15 when I decided my big-time goals lay within the modelling industry, with only about four years of experience up my sleeve. It wasn't a whole lot to lean back on. I took out a pen and paper and created a list of what I needed to do to get myself from A to B to C, and so on. The list was a map, in a way, helping me visualise and plan the next few years.

I am, by the way, the queen of lists and notes. I write notes on everything, everywhere: in diaries, notepads, on the fridge, in my phone, on my laptop. My notes are planted all over the house at all times. Writing things down keeps me accountable. If it's in black and white, I have to make it happen. The best thing about a list is the satisfaction I feel when I cross things off. When I can physically see on paper what I've completed, I get a real rush of happiness and momentum.

Finding financial independence

Building your career is amazing. The independence that comes with earning your own money is so freeing! I started off working in a café after school and on the weekends for extra cash: eleven bucks an hour! The boss was so awful. He'd yell at us all constantly to the point where I'd cry — which is big, because I do not cry often. I stuck it out though because I knew it wasn't forever.

When it came to modelling, I set my sights on working with the types of clients I aspired to: the photographers, stylists, other models, etc. I didn't focus as much on the money side of things because before you can expect to earn good money, you have to develop a good reputation and learn the ropes. Also, I was too busy trying to stay focused and avoid getting caught up in all that was going on around me to think about pay cheques.

Excitement kicks in when you're doing something you love. You get a surge of energy to go, go, go! But learning to be composed and polished is truly important. Try to avoid doing lots of half-hearted things just to say 'I did it' and you'll feel better in the long run. Deep down, you always know when you're rushing and not giving 100 percent. Getting in the habit of completing things properly from the get-go will lead to a flourishing professional reputation.

Four likely outcomes from a casting:

1. I book the job. This is of course my favourite outcome!

2. I get close, but not close enough. I might get a call back or I'll be popped on hold, but in the end the client will go for another model.

3. I never hear back from the client. This is painfully frustrating, but it happens so it's best to be prepared.

4. I book the job but the client will promise the world and never pull through with the goods. This is the worst outcome by far as it's so disheartening. I tackle this outcome by holding my excitement in until the dotted line is signed. Although I still have a positive outlook, it allows me to avoid unnecessary disappointment.

When it comes to earning an income, remember that everyone has to start at square one. Again, it's not a race. Spend quality time focusing on your skills and expertise. From there, trust that your income will grow over time.

P is for positive

As I mentioned, in the beginning of my career, eliminating the fear factor was high on my to-do list. To achieve this, I decided to adopt and maintain a positive mindset. I began reading about the power of positive thinking and how beneficial it is for your career as well as your mental health.

Adopting a positive mindset meant remembering that old saying, 'the glass is half full,' rather than 'the glass is half empty'. Looking at things this way means that I approach every day and every situation positively. It might sound corny or like a cliché, but it's far from it. Before you write it off, think of it this way: the most amazing part of a positive mindset is that you start to notice the silver lining in everything. Bad days won't look so bad if you can approach life with a positive attitude.

In the modelling world, for example, I now go into every casting with a rational, positive mindset. Instead of becoming nervous and getting my undies in a twist, I break down the situation so it's clear and I'm prepared. In my case, castings usually end with one of four likely outcomes:

LET'S MAKE 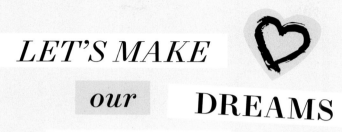 *our* **DREAMS** *come true.*

LET'S HAVE

F U N

LET'S LIVE *our lives happily together* *FOREVER.*

Extract from Elyse's diary, 2013

Breaking things down like this means I waste less headspace storing a million 'What if?' thoughts. Without all the worry, there is stacks of room for positive thoughts. I'm able to see that no matter what the outcome, something good will come out of the experience, whether it's meeting a designer or photographer, forming a relationship with a casting agent or getting to know other models. This kind of positive thinking means that I skip the feeling of disappointment. And if I end up booking the job, then that's an added bonus.

I've also stopped ignoring my 'little wins' along the way. For example, getting a casting in the first place is in itself a win! Wins are wins no matter their size. People forget that many little wins can add up to a prize bigger than ever anticipated.

ACHIEVING YOUR DREAM IS NO ONE'S RESPONSIBILITY BUT YOUR OWN.

A little sacrifice goes a long way

Working your way up also involves being willing to make sacrifices. I had to sacrifice a lot during my teenage years especially. As I was only 15 when my modelling career became more serious, I was still in high school. I had three very important years to go. There was no way I was going to quit school as your education should be priority numero uno, so I accepted the circumstances and made it work. Achieving your dream is no one's responsibility but your own.

During those last three years of school, there were many days and countless classes where I'd have to leave early to make my call time. Some kids might have thought I was lucky to miss all that school, but trust me, I wasn't. I'd miss instructions, explanations and plain old learning time, which was a massive blow as it made the task of maintaining my grades tough, though not impossible.

It took me a while to figure out the juggling act, but I soon got the hang of it. It meant getting up earlier in the mornings and staying up later to finish homework. I was lucky to have Dad by my side the whole way. Dad would sit down with me and go through my notes to make sure I was keeping up.

Leaning on those you love for support and encouragement is not a sign of weakness; it's an essential part of success.

Weekends were dedicated to working on my modelling portfolio, so my social life narrowed. I did, however, play competitive tennis every Saturday morning. I was pretty good and I loved it, but it meant I had to squeeze in training during my already very crammed weeks. Having a physical outlet when you're working super hard is an amazing form of rejuvenation. If you're exercising to unwind it might not feel like you are 'resting', but you're giving your brain some timeout, which can be as important as sleep.

Going to movies, shopping and late-night partying, on the other hand, were big no-nos. The partying bit didn't faze me all that much as it kept me on the healthier side, but at times it was tough saying no to friends and invitations so I could stay home and study. My big-picture goal was firmly nestled in my mind, though, and that always kept me going. I've always really looked forward to my dream becoming my reality. Determination is like a superpower: incredibly motivating.

By the time I finished high school, I had a great finishing score and good relationships with my teachers. My modelling career had become more stable and showed lots of potential. After three years of constant prioritising and working my butt off, I was ready to take on adult life, all guns blazing!

From that point on I had the gift of time and, to this day, I do not take time for granted. Every day is an opportunity to move further towards my goal. Every day is a gift. Don't hide behind thoughts like, 'I'll get to that tomorrow,' or 'That can wait'. There is no time like the present.

Slogging it out only feels tough in the moment. Just like a workout, the pain is short term! When you push yourself to hold on for those last few seconds, the rush of endorphins is much greater. Be strong. You are capable of anything you put your mind to.

Five key lessons
I've learnt over my career

1 **FIND PEOPLE WHO INSPIRE YOU.**
Finding people who inspire you is a special way of learning. Even if you don't know them personally, you can learn so much by reading books they have written or articles they've been featured in. YouTube and podcasts are also fantastic resources.

Growing up, I had two major figures of inspiration, who continue to inspire me to this day: Miranda Kerr and Elle Macpherson. Both of these women are not only beautiful, but also strong, smart and driven. They have enormous modelling careers, thriving business ventures, have lived around the globe and, to top it all off, are working mums. Now those are some résumés!

Miranda was dropped into the industry after winning a *Dolly* magazine competition and has since appeared on the covers of international *Vogue, ELLE, Harper's Bazaar* and more. She's walked for Prada and Chanel and, in 2007, was offered a contract with Victoria's Secret, which is mega.

Elle's career is iconic. Not only has she graced the cover of everything from *Vogue* to *Sports Illustrated*, Elle has also launched her own businesses and raised two beautiful sons. Elle is known as 'the Body', but to me she's 'the Powerhouse' — strong both mentally and physically.

2 BE KIND, BE HUMBLE.

Kindness will take you a long way. I don't have much patience anymore for arrogant, nasty people. I've come across my fair share and it's safe to say that I am well and truly done. If you get a bad name (in my industry especially), it's unlikely a client will rebook you. And word travels, no matter how gorgeous you might be.

Most modelling jobs are big productions that involve a lot of people. My rule is that every single person on the shoot — the photographer, the make-up artist, another model, a caterer, an intern — is equally important. Everyone should be treated with respect. We're all there to work on a mutual goal, so without one person the ship goes down. At the start of a shoot, I'll introduce myself to everyone on set. Then when we wrap up for the day, I'll give everyone a big high-five to thank them for their efforts.

In the working world, we all have to start at the bottom. We've all experienced the first day of a new job where we don't know the lay of the land. We've all made mistakes and had days when we think the boss is about ready to kill us. Use these memories to be kind, patient and compassionate. You don't want to be feared — life is too short.

The Block was a huge eye opener for Josh and me. We like to surround ourselves with kind-hearted, genuine people. *The Block* throws you into a situation where you're living and working with people you've never met before and with whom you might not see eye to eye. To cap it off, there are many days when you are working off no sleep.

Pressure, exhaustion and competitiveness can drive people to their worst, and they can forget the benefits of being kind. Yes, some things in life are competitive but, at the end of the day, helping someone today means they're more likely to help you tomorrow. Plus, karma is a nightmare. Keep your conscience healthy.

Lastly, don't let people stifle your potential. People should celebrate your potential, just as you should celebrate theirs.

3 TAKE YOURSELF SERIOUSLY.

Modelling is a highly competitive industry, as are many others. From the get-go you have to present yourself professionally and prove that you have what it takes to do a great job.

When I rock up to a job, whether it's a cover or a catalogue, I make absolutely sure that I am in shape, my skin is clean, I'm on time (if not early) and I take the time to introduce myself to the whole team. If there is anything on my mind, or something is stressing me out, I park those distracting thoughts and concentrate on the job at hand. If something happens to be troubling me and my phone is likely to remind me of it during a job (via a text message or email), I bench my phone for the day. I don't let anything but professionalism appear in front of the camera, as it captures both the physical and the emotional.

Take yourself seriously and act professionally, and people will treat you that way as well.

4 CELEBRATE THAT PART OF YOU THAT IS UNIQUE.

I love reminding people that there is only one of you. Do your best to quit the comparisons. Yes, she might have this, and they might have that, but you have something unique as well. Own whatever it is that makes you stand out — and cherish it.

Being totally comfortable in your own skin is not made any easier by social media. But the beauty is that you have the power to log off, shut down or switch off. I have a digital detox every few days and it is bliss. Life is there to be lived, after all, not scrolled through.

5 WRITE LISTS AND COMMIT TO BEING A DO-ER.

As I've claimed a few times, I'm the queen of lists and notes. Every few weeks, I block time out to sit down, write down a list of goals and then work out what it's going to take to get myself there. If it's a huge goal, I'll break it down into smaller parts and take it step by step or day by day.

As I am doing this, I get out the last list of goals and cross off everything I've achieved. Give yourself a second to pat yourself on the back and feel proud of what you've done! Celebrations along the way are a crucial part of maintaining motivation and momentum.

YOU ARE UNIQUE.

It's taken me a long time to get comfortable with the idea that I don't have to change for anyone.

THE KNOWLES FAMILY

Meet my Dad, Stuart

THE KING OF THE KNOWLES FAMILY

I look at Dad and laugh. He always has a smile on his face, like he's ready to chuckle. Dad has brought us kids up to be true and genuine. Love you, Dad!

Dad taught us the meaning of hard work — and how to have a bloody good time!

Elyse speaks so highly of you. You've taught her some crucial life lessons and raised a very hard-working, grounded girl. What is it that makes her so gutsy and outrageously driven?

Elyse's guts and determination are driven by her sheer desire to constantly learn and improve. She wants to be at her best and she absolutely loves to prove people wrong. The sky is the limit. As long as you work hard to achieve your goals, anything is possible.

Enough of the sentimental stuff for a quick second. Tell us about a time when you thought to yourself, 'Where did that sweet, polished model go?'

The polished model goes out the door when she is sitting around the camp fire, acting like her true-blue Aussie self!

It's great to see her fun, laid-back character really shine through when she has some time off and time to herself. When she's around her old friends, her barriers come down and the outgoing Elyse really comes out.

Can you summarise Elyse in a collection of words?

Loving, driven, passionate, artistic and ambitious.

CHAPTER FOUR

Modelling

As I say often in this book, there is only one of you in this world. Your unique qualities, look and personality are special and it's important to embrace them. Quit trying to be like everyone else on Instagram and in magazines and focus on being your best self. It's amazing how beautiful and confident you will feel if you own who you are. Nothing is more exquisite than self-confidence.

Keep going. Keep pushing.

The modelling world has been my life for many years and I absolutely love it: the work, the travel, the people I meet and the opportunities that present themselves along the way. Throughout this chapter I'll offer pieces of advice from my experiences. As with many careers, in modelling your most important quality is self-confidence. You need to be able to wholeheartedly back yourself as it's a highly competitive industry. Respect your body by keeping fit and well nourished, and you absolutely need to trust that gut of yours. Be wise when making decisions and avoid allowing people to push you around. If you can strengthen your self-confidence and learn to be comfortable in your own skin as early in your career as possible, you shouldn't have anything to fear.

Other important qualities are resilience, patience, hard work and a thick skin. Knock-backs will happen. People may look past you from time to time and, much to your frustration, some doors will close. Just keep telling yourself: 'When one door closes, another will open'. Keep going. Keep pushing.

Working on set

Being on a fashion shoot with a full production team is one of my favourite environments. It's important to be versatile and feel comfortable in swim, ready-to-wear (casual and street styles), lingerie and high-end editorial looks. Shooting on a beach in bathers is beautiful, but working with high-end pieces is special too. When I'm styled in an extravagant look, a new sense of confidence comes out. It's amazing how fashion can change the way you feel.

The stylist is the expert when it comes to creating incredible looks, though given that I know my body shape so well, it can be helpful to have a little input before the shoot gets going. It's not about dictating what I want to wear, but about making sure the stylist has all of the information he or she needs to create the best result for the client. For example, as much as I love styles that sit low on the hips or finish just below the knee, they do not do me or the clothing any favours. Wanting to look and feel your best does not have to be about vanity. It's about saving the stylist from wasting their efforts on looks that will not match their vision.

WANTING TO LOOK AND FEEL YOUR BEST DOES NOT HAVE TO BE ABOUT VANITY.

Chatting to stylists can also lead to ideas they might never have considered prior to getting to know you. If you're a model, don't be afraid to talk to the team. You're just as much a part of the creative family as anyone else. And make sure to speak up if you're not feeling okay. If you're not comfortable, it'll show in the shots.

I get to work with amazing stylists on shoots and witness their unique techniques. The stylists always bring colour and life to a set. They roll in racks of beautiful clothing, line the floor with shoes and accessories and fill the room with big personalities and lots of character. Typically, they'll interact with the photographer and the hair and make-up artists to ensure they are on the same page. It's

Your voice is there for a reason, so don't be afraid to use it.

important that the whole team is united and cohesive.

I love the build up of noise when I'm on a shoot. Music normally plays, the flash of the camera clicks away in the background as the lighting is tested, people yell out from one side of the room to the other. A shoot is usually a hub of life and creation. I watch everyone do their thing and get involved as much as possible. There is so much to learn on a shoot and so many people to meet.

Creating good relationships is important and getting to know designers and exploring their ranges each season is a big part of my job. If you work in fashion or are aiming to wriggle in, you may have heard the saying, 'It's not about what you know, but who you know'. This doesn't mean you need to be best friends with the editors of *Vogue* and *Harper's* or all the top PR people. It simply means that putting an effort into getting to know people can lead to opportunities. You don't have to put on a charade or chew off their ears. Simple manners are the key and are so often forgotten. Introducing yourself and asking about the other person before talking about yourself is good manners and good research. I've made close friends at events and photo shoots. One minute they're styling me or fixing my hair, the next we're out skating together!

Modelling interstate and overseas

Travel can be a big part of modelling. It feels like I've been to Sydney a million times in the last few years as most magazines are based there. Commuting can be exhausting, but music, a good book and healthy snacks make travel a breeze. Quick tip: always take the stairs when you have the option in the airport.

I only ever go to Sydney for a few days at a time, so packing is easy. I never travel without a strapless bra (essential for 99 percent of my jobs), runners, workout gear and one outfit that I can dress up or down by changing the top and my shoes. Carrying two tops is also a good idea in case I spill something, which happens.

Overseas travel is also important. I have an agent in Los Angeles, as the market there is a good fit for me. Trying to get to the U.S. once a year has to be a priority. Growing and maintaining relationships around the world is key to growth. If you want to go global, do the groundwork in as many cities as you can.

Steps to kick-start a modelling career

For anyone who is interested in modelling, here are some tips to point you in the right direction. If an agency signs you, congratulations! From that point on, learning to be patient is the next hurdle. Things in this industry take time. Use the time to gain experience and to work on yourself. Sometimes things won't turn out the way you wished, but remember that at least you gave it a go. That alone is a huge personal accomplishment.

1 Research agencies in your area. Either Google them or have a chat to friends and family. It's a good idea to approach a few different agencies rather than just one. They'll all be on the lookout for different looks at different times, so try to meet as many as you can.

2 When you approach an agency, you can either email photos or pop into their agency in person. It's best to check online to see when their office is open as usually they'll specify an hour or two in the afternoon to go in.

If you visit an agency, feel free to bring a parent or a guardian (especially if you're under 18). Be prepared for the agent to take some photos of you using a digital camera and to take your measurements.

3 If you email photos, the photos should not be professional, so don't spend a penny. Simply ask a parent or a friend to take some photos of you using their iPhone or a digital camera.

Pop on some fitted jeans, a singlet and heels to show off

Patience is the key.

your beautiful shape. Agencies will want to see the real you, so when it comes to make-up all you need is a light base, mascara, lip balm and maybe a touch of bronzer. Aim for six photos if you can: a few taken from the front, a few from the side and include a few different crops (full body, close up, and so on). Posing is not a must. Just stand tall, look confident and throw in at least one big smile!

4 Measurements are not essential at this point, but if you want to be super organised, grab a tape measure and jot them down for your height, bust, waist and hips. Once you have all of this, send your details to at least two to four agencies, depending on how many are in your area. If you visit in person, be yourself: confident and strong. If it's a no, don't let this get you

down. It's common for models to approach lots of different agencies before the right fit comes along.

If the first agency you see wants to sign you on the spot, I suggest you thank them and say you need a few days to think about everything presented. It's important to see all of the possible agencies before making your selection. When it comes to modelling, go with the agency/agent where you feel most comfortable.

5 All agencies come with a contract. This shouldn't scare you; a modelling contract is standard. If you are handed one, never sign it on the spot. Take the contract home to read with someone else. There is no rush.

A few tips around signing a contract

It's natural for excitement to take over when an agency wants to sign you. It's such a happy moment and one you should absolutely celebrate, but remember to keep calm while going over the agency contract. I have a lawyer read over any contract before I sign because I'd rather be safe than sorry. Start your career with a strong foundation to avoid unwanted surprises down the road.

* Have a parent, guardian or someone else you trust and who is knowledgeable in this area read it with you (even if you are over 18).
* Avoid signing anything that locks you in for a set period of time. Occasionally agencies say 12 months, which is okay, but make sure you have the freedom to leave when you want to.
* Don't be afraid to ask questions if you're confused or feel unsure. Remember, your agency is there to help build, guide and support you and your career. Don't let a contract scare you away. Read it carefully until you feel totally aware of what it means. Go with the agency that you trust and feel most comfortable with.
* Look out for red flags — meaning, anything that seems unusual or doesn't sit well with you. If you are unsure or uncomfortable about anything, be assertive and ask advice from a parent, another adult experienced with contracts or even other models. Some common red flags include:

  - paying up-front fees to an agency
  - contracts that lock you into the agency for more than 12 months
  - agencies that take more than a 20 percent commission.

Once the contract is signed, congratulations! You're in for an amazing ride, so stop and enjoy the moment.

As in any job, there is a lot to learn. One important thing to work on is personal organisation. Get into the habit of using a diary to write everything down so you don't forget arrangements, call and wrap times or other specifications. I keep an old-school paper diary, but your phone is another good option. Also, get used to Google Maps. You never know where a shoot might take you, and rocking up late and frazzled is less than ideal.

A collection of my
modelling photos from
over the years. It's
fun looking back on the
earlier days.

Modelling glossary

There is a bit of 'modelling lingo', so to get you started here are some of the main terms. Never be afraid to call your agent when you come across something you don't understand. They're there for you.

Call back/recall

After your first casting, if the client wants to see you again you'll get a recall (a second casting). Sometimes you might even get a third, depending on the job.

Call sheet

A call sheet is a document you'll receive from your agent prior to a job, listing the date, time, location and contact information. Be sure to save a copy on your phone. It's a good idea to read the entire call sheet rather than just your personal call time. Getting to know the creative team before rocking up on the day seems both polite and respectful.

Call time/ wrap time

Your 'call time' is the time when you need to rock up to a shoot. Your 'wrap time' is when you're scheduled to finish. It's not uncommon for shoots to go over time, so it's important to call your agent and tell him or her the minute you finish up.

Comp card

Formally known as a 'composite card', a comp card is a model's version of a business card. Your agency will create one and print it for you. A comp card typically includes four to five of your strongest shots, your measurements and your agency's contact details.

Comp cards go with you everywhere. Keep them in your portfolio, in your car, in your diary — you never know when a casting might pop up.

Digitals

These are photos taken by your agency using a digital camera (nothing super fancy). Your digital photos show you in your natural state: very little make-up, clean hair and dressed in fitted jeans, a singlet and heels.

If you shoot swim and lingerie, it's important to include some shots of you wearing either/or. Digitals should be updated by your agent every few months (especially if you change your hair or grow a lot taller) as they show clients your most recent self. Don't be afraid of digitals. Your bare and natural self is you at your most beautiful.

Go-sees

These are when your agency sets up a series of meet-and-greets for you with a range of clients. Usually each go-see is just five to fifteen minutes long, so squeeze in as many as you can on one day to be efficient. Your personality is a big element of go-sees. Bring a smile, a positive attitude and your best manners.

Model fees

Depending on the job, your model fee will usually be split into two components: photographic fees and usage fees. Photographic fees refer to your time in front of the camera (i.e., the actual shoot day). Usage fees refer to how, where and for how long your images will be used. For example, if your photo is to be featured in a magazine and in store windows, on a billboard or in a TV commercial, you'll usually be paid additionally.

Model kit

This is what you take to each job — like a gym bag, but for modelling jobs. Normally your agent will tell you if you need anything specific, but I have a basic list I bring to almost every shoot. Get into the habit of going to all jobs with clean hair, a clean face, fresh nails and your model kit.

Model placement

Travelling as a model is very common. If you and your agency decide that it's a good idea for you to model in another city for a period of time, this is called a 'placement'. Your agency will 'place' you with another agency in a chosen city.

Mother agency

It's common for a model to be signed to multiple agencies around the world at the same time. Each model, however, should always have one central mother agency or manager. Your mother agency is typically based in your home city. Your mother agency will place you with other agencies around the world and will continue to be your best point of contact.

Portfolio

This is essentially an album of your best work. Your agency will prepare it for you, so when they place the photos in a particular order, it's a good idea to leave it be. They know their clients and they know the industry. Trusting your agent is important.

Request casting/ cattle casting

A casting is when a client meets a bunch of models for an upcoming shoot or campaign. If a client asks to see you, specifically, it is referred to as a 'request casting'. If a client asks to see a range of models who fit a particular criteria, it is a 'cattle casting'.

Both types of castings are equally important. Be prompt and on time. If you miss your time, you might not get a second shot. Castings are usually go, go, go!

Test shoot

This is a photo shoot that's not for a client, but simply for your own experience and portfolio. Test shoots are great for improving your movement, your confidence and learning about camera angles and lighting. You can play around with poses, get a feel for different locations (outside and studio) and, of course, different fashions.

Usually the cost of a test shoot falls on the model, so make sure you're not being ripped off. Your agency will guide you through it. Test shoots are an important investment, so if you can, aim for at least a few per year.

Shooting my absolute dream job: Seafolly, on the iconic
Bondi Beach. I worked so hard for years and years to
land this ambassadorship.

PHOTOS © HANNAH SCOTT-STEVENSON

I'll never forget this campaign shoot.

What is in my model kit?

The life of a model tends to be on-the-go. Make sure
your bag is always fully equipped.

Clothing and shoes

* Nude G
* Strapless bra
* Nipple covers
* Heels and a casual
  flat shoe — for moving
  around during the day,
  riding in cars to different
  locations, etc.

Organisation

* Diary and pen —
  I love taking notes.
  I always learn
  something new
  on a shoot.

Hair

* Hair brush
* Hair ties — clients and
  photographers normally
  want hair-up and hair-
  down options, so it's a
  good idea to have some
  with you.

Make-up

* Lip gloss
* Lipstick
* Powder
* Touch-up kit — going
  between castings all day
  can feel rushed. You'll
  feel better if you can
  freshen up once or twice
  with concealer, powder,
  bronzer and lipstick.

Promotion

* Portfolio on an
  iPad as it's easy
  to edit.
* Comp cards

Personal care

* Deodorant and a small
  perfume — so you
  smell fresh.
* Eye drops — eyes can
  become dry or red (my
  eyes are always red!)
  when you travel or shoot
  in bright conditions.

84

Q&A
MUSES & INSPIRATION

Lana Wilkinson

Lana Wilkinson is the definition of
a pocket rocket. A highly sought-after
Australian stylist, Lana sparkles with charm,
class and magnificent style.

Q. In your view, what are the five key wardrobe essentials?

A. Style is not fashion. Stylish people use fashion, but fashion has its place. Style is empowering when you understand your limits and strengths, and know how to exploit them favourably. When it comes to your personal look, it's not permanent — it can be changed, tweaked and recreated when you have the key essentials in your wardrobe. My key must-haves are:

1. Denim jeans These are the wardrobe staple. Fit and wash are everything. If you're going to invest in anything, invest in a good pair of jeans. Denim jeans can take you from day to night with a simple shoe, blouse or jacket change. They are the lazy girl's holy grail. No matter what your style — boot cut, skinny or straight leg — invest in denim that you can wear all day, every day.

2. White shirt/T-shirt This is not your school uniform white shirt or work shirt. The fabric and cut are key. White is my go-to colour and adds a level of effortlessness and ease to any outfit. Try it with an embellished skirt, jewelled earrings and heels for a smart-casual dress code.

It doesn't get any more classic than a white T-shirt. The best styles are super-soft and have a relaxed, lived-in fit. A crewneck cut is a no-brainer, but I also like a V-neck style because it's a little bit sexier and the perfect canvas for layering necklaces.

3. Black blazer A good black blazer will never go out of fashion and there is one to suit any budget. Broad-shoulder blazers highlight a small waist and also lengthen your body. You can show off your sexy side with a black tuxedo and crisp shirt or, for evening, a nice black bra peeping through can take the blazer from day to play. Tone down the severity of the classic black blazer with low-key separates like a T-shirt or worn-in jeans. Avoid wearing it with workwear shift dresses unless heading into the office.

4. Black pumps When it comes to shoes, black pumps are perhaps the most reliable and versatile option. They're perfectly suited for almost any outfit and occasion.

5. The little black dress There's a reason why the little black dress (LBD) is the most valuable item in your wardrobe. It's appropriate for many situations, particularly those unplanned, last-minute occasions. It will save you every time. Dressed up with heels or dressed down with flats or sneakers — and co-ordinating accessories — its possibilities are limitless.

Q. When it's time to invest in denim, any tips for finding a good fit?

A. Finding a good pair of jeans can be like finding the perfect swimsuit: emotionally exhausting but rewarding when you find the perfect pair. Best of all, there are various brands and styles available to suit everyone's budget.

My top tips are:

1. Understand your body proportions

Buying denim is deeply personal because you are confronting your body shape. But it's not just about shape. It's about understanding the parts of your body you wish to highlight:

— If you are long in the torso with short legs, you need a high waist to give you 'more' leg length.

— If you have a short body with long legs, a mid-rise waist is going to look best on you to define your waist.

2. Fit is key The biggest mistake women make is wearing jeans too big, which makes them look larger than they really are. You should spend a minute wriggling into them. Think of them as shape wear and only go up a size if you are breaking a sweat while standing still. That age-old theory that denim stretches is true!

3. Know your style You shouldn't force yourself to be a boot cut, skinny or flare girl unless the style suits you. Jeans shouldn't be about making a fashion statement; jeans are timeless. Some of your favourite celebrities may wear the same style of jeans day in and day out because in this case, different isn't necessarily better.

Q. When you take on a new client, do you do research and match your styling to her personality? Or do you style based on her look and shape?

A. It's definitely a combination. Research is key when taking on a new client. I look at their current style profile on Instagram or online. I'll then chat to my client prior to a fitting to understand what styles she likes and what she likes and dislikes about her body shape.

My client's personality is a big consideration. It's my job to extract what the client likes and dislikes about themselves and then consider what fashion looks or trends will work best. It is essential to collaborate with your client and for them to feel the best of themselves, rather than be something they are not. When you feel your best, you look your best and that is contagious. Trust is key. Standing in front of someone and sharing your fears about your body is a deeply personal thing, a responsibility I take very seriously.

It's a simple formula. For example, if you have a great décolletage and arms, play those up. If it's your legs you love, show those instead. Colour, proportion and even your attitude can make all the difference. To be successful as a stylist, you need to embrace the individual and let their personality shine.

All that said, the talent has come to me for a reason, so I ensure my sense of style and experience is reflected in the end look. That's why collaborating with my clients is important — you build the trust from the outset. We then go on a journey together.

Q. Fashion can be expensive. How can we save money yet still keep up with trends?

A. When it comes to your key wardrobe essentials, invest in quality over quantity. Spend money on key designer items like bags, shoes and sunglasses during sale periods so you get more for your money. When purchasing trend pieces, look to fast-fashion high street outlets to ensure you don't overcapitalise on something that may no longer be in fashion in six months. This, combined with your wardrobe essentials, will see you looking on-trend and fashion forward.

Q. Fashion is one thing, comfort is another. Any tips for making an evening look more comfortable for long days and nights?

A. Being comfortable is all about how you feel — literally and emotionally. Whether it's your dress, your underwear or your shoes, make sure you consider fit and weather conditions and be sure to take a photo of yourself before you head out, so you are comfortable with how you look. Also, remember that your hair and make-up

are your best accessories.

Wear good functional underwear to highlight your best assets. Ensure your bra fits you well. It makes your clothes look better, which makes you feel better, which makes you more comfortable. Shape wear is an easy go-to as it's comfortable and also hides some of the things we perhaps don't like.

Comfortable feet are key to the longevity of your night. If you're like me and like high shoes, keep foot gels in your bag so you can dance the night away. If that's not for you, select a shoe that is closed in the back and/or has a block heel for additional support. Flats and sneakers can also be very cool.

Finally, be aware of the weather conditions. Whether it's a trench coat, faux fur or blazer, a jacket is always good to take with you if it's the difference between having a good night or a bad night.

'When you feel your best, you look your best and that is contagious.'

—Lana Wilkinson

CHAPTER FIVE

Health & Wellness

I f anyone reading this chapter is wearing something uncomfortable or is still in work clothes, heels or make-up or if you are tired, grumpy, stressed or bloated, then first things first: go and have a warm shower, wash your face, pop on something comfy and then come back to me when you are feeling fresh, restored and (best of all) naturally you.

Okay, are you back? I bet many of you never left. C'mon ... off you go! You'll feel better for it, I promise.

Cherish your natural self

I am *trusting* that you left and are now back feeling refreshed. Right in this moment you should feel a little calmer, lighter and less distracted. Right? It's because you are now 100 percent you. You are the very best version of yourself because you are comfortable, stripped back and natural. Keep this feeling in mind. This is the feeling you want to carry with you for every step in every day.

One thing I am trying to do more of is give my body the chance to completely retreat back to its natural state, to my natural self. Doing this more often lifts my energy levels and my confidence because I am not wasting time feeling negative or uncomfortable. I can't hide behind anything if I am bare. I'm forced to just be me and to find comfort and peace in this. If you can try to do this as well, I swear you'll notice a difference.

I know it's easy to say and hard to feel at times, but in our natural state we are absolutely perfect. We don't need make-up or labels to feel good. We don't need to look around at what she has or what they have. There is no point doing this because the reality is we're all completely different. Each one of us is a unique individual. If you can find the courage to be grateful and proud of who you are and what you have, a shift will occur. Positive energy will flood your body.

If you can find this sense of confidence, cherish it and silence anything else from spoiling the moment. Confidence is silent; insecurities are loud. Don't worry about others, especially people who seem jealous or never have a nice word to say. Jealously is the biggest form of insecurity. Instead, surround yourself with great people and get to know your strengths, weaknesses, limits and boundaries, what makes you happy and what pushes your buttons. The best way to do this is to be guided by your own experiences.

Just be

Health and wellness are among my favourite things to write about because they're two of my favourite aspects of life. I invest so much time into keeping fit and strong, preparing nutritious meals, snacks and smoothies and, of course, making sure that every single day I dedicate a period of time to just be.

Just 'being' could mean anything from switching my phone off for a few hours and taking Isla for a walk to reading a book, finding a sunny café to have a chai latte, listening to music or even meditating. Whatever form of 'being' I choose for the day, it's a time when I let my body and brain focus on nothing but breathing and the present moment. It took me a while to learn how to do this. To be honest, I used to think it was lazy and a waste of time. I couldn't have been more wrong. This time is my haven.

My days are always varied and never quite predictable. I spend a lot of time travelling. I train a fair bit and I work hard. To some, modelling might mean smiling for the camera, but it is much more than that. To me, modelling means building a brand with a well-rounded, dynamic and hard-working business behind it. Taking timeout is an essential part of resting, as important as sleep. Turning away from distractions and switching your thoughts to mute gives your mind and body a chance to recharge, sharpen up and rejuvenate. Things become clearer, decisions become easier and your attitude slowly starts to play in a more positive field.

Looking for positive patterns

I'm not an expert when it comes to food and nutrition, fitness or mindfulness and mental strength, but I have tried a bunch of different things in all three categories over time and can share with you my personal experiences. Plus I'll let you in on a few helpful and healthy habits I've picked up over the years.

When it comes to my body and mind, the most basic thing I do is look for consistent patterns that lead to positive outcomes. Now as with most things in life, you have to be patient to find these patterns. There isn't much that happens in a blink of an eye, overnight or even after a few days. Most great things in life come after weeks, months and years of continuous trial and effort. The 'effort factor' is key. You, and only you, are in complete control of how much effort you put into whatever you're doing.

We are all different in many ways. Our bodies, our strengths and weaknesses, our sources of motivation and our genetics. When it comes to staying in shape, keeping fit and becoming faster and stronger, what works for some isn't going to work for all. We've all heard this before (many, many times!) so my take on this idea is simple: if I see or read about something that appeals to me, such as a new workout, I try it. I slot it into my diary for the next few weeks and/or months and simply see what happens. Over those weeks or months, I keep my eye on two things:

1. How do I feel, physically and mentally?
Is it straining my back or hurting my knees? Is it giving me more or less endorphins than what I'm used to?

2. Is my new habit leading to consistent and positive outcomes?
Has my fitness level maintained itself or am I getting progressively fitter each week/month? If I cut out fruit, does my gut feel less bloated or is it the same as always? If I increase the amount of protein I eat at dinner, do I notice a change in my energy levels?

Again, patience is important. Ask yourself the above questions and look for patterns that have led to good results. Just make sure you have genuinely given whatever you are trying a red-hot crack over a realistic period of time.

Food

To me, food is about fuelling your mind and body. Food is about getting together with your loved ones and sharing a meal. Food is about culture. Most of all, food is about allowing your body to feel energetic, fresh and well nourished. Having a good relationship with food can make the world of difference to your mood, so ditch the guilt and feed your body kindly.

If I lack energy, my mood is low or I'm flat-out grumpy, I stick to ... fresh fruit. Fruit is a great source of natural sugar that turns into the particular energy I lack on days like these. Eating fruit helps me refuel. It also fights off the cravings that haunt so many of us when we're in a grump, such as for lollies and other processed sugars.

Having said this, I am not super-duper strict 100 percent of the time as I work out pretty aggressively throughout the week and I believe in moderation. Of course our pantry has some treats inside and I occasionally allow myself to eat them. Chocolate is a dear old friend of mine — we go way back. But we certainly don't catch up every day!

Right now (in fact, as I write this), I'm drinking lemon and ginger kombucha. Kombucha is a naturally fermented drink that helps with digestion, gut health and mood stability. I love the taste and find that it's a great way to trick your tastebuds into thinking you're having something naughty.

If I'm feeling low and I am tempted to pull the plug on my morning alarm, I'm quick to make sure this doesn't happen. Sleeping through a workout because of a grumpy mood brings out the real beast: regret. So the night before my workout, I eat a big dinner of fresh fish (usually salmon) with roasted veggies or a yummy beetroot, goat's cheese, pumpkin, quinoa, toasted almonds and spinach salad. Dinners like this mean I wake up feeling light instead of heavy, sluggish and slow.

I understand salmon and veggies aren't for everyone. After lots of reading, cooking and eating, I've found that when it comes to dinners that make you feel full, fresh and happy, the absolute failproof combination is a good portion of protein with a side of anything fresh from the garden.

Chicken, fish (including tuna), pork, lean cuts of beef, eggs and

Never underestimate the power of a well-balanced diet.

Wholesome, filling and nutritious foods can change my mood in a second.

MY SHOPPING LIST ALWAYS INCLUDES …

* Spinach leaves
* Beetroot
* Pumpkin
* Cauliflower
* Zucchini
* Avocado
* Broccoli
* Sweet potato
* Beans
* Red onion
* Lemons
* Ginger
* Bananas
* Apples
* Blueberries and raspberries
* Salmon
* Chicken
* Fresh fish
* Meat from the butcher
* Natural healthy dips
* Crackers
* Free-range eggs
* Muesli (raw)
* Almond milk
* Regular milk for Josh
* Whole Greek yoghurt
* Goat's cheese — my personal favourite
* Chai
* Wraps

tofu are all good options. Then add a rainbow of colour. I start with leafy greens and from there just chuck in what I like. Personally, avocado and beetroot fill me up and tomatoes gross me out!

When it comes to adding extra flavour to my salad or vegetables, I stick to fresh herbs, lemon or lime, olive oil and/or a sprinkle of salt and pepper. For a super easy and yummy dressing, add a few tablespoons each of lemon juice, tahini (which adds a nutty flavour) and sesame oil into a bowl with a little bit of honey for sweetness and whisk it until the flavour is right for you. Or even easier, try red wine vinegar on your salad. Keep it clean and wake up feeling energised.

I work out first thing in the morning and save my breakfast till after. This works for me because ... if I eat right before a workout, I tend to get stitches. Instead, I train early and head home for my favourite meal of the day: breakfast.

At the moment, my brekkie consists of a bowl of whole Greek yoghurt, raw muesli and blueberries — super quick, simple and packed with goodness.

When I have a little more time in the morning and my pantry is properly stocked, I make a smoothie bowl. Inside the blender I mix almond milk, cocoa, greens, banana and maca, protein powders and cinnamon. I then pour it into a bowl and sprinkle raw granola (meaning, granola that hasn't been toasted) over the top. It is so yummy it's hard to believe that it's good for you. If I am craving something savoury, I'll go for three eggs scrambled (I don't add milk) with spinach in a pan. When it's on my plate, I add avocado, goat's cheese and pesto on top. Delicious and packed full of protein and nutrients.

On a cheat day, my go-to treat is ... Reese's Peanut Butter Cups. Josh always knows exactly when I need one! Usually it's when I am the crankiest girl alive.

The one food that has never agreed with my skin is ... lollies. I used to be a huge lolly girl growing up, but I started to see the effects on my skin. Now I do everything possible to protect my skin because I've had so many problems. Goodbye lollies.

In my opinion, the worst thing you can do when it comes to your diet is ... skip meals. I don't think it's a good idea to teach your body to cope with being starved. Your body is smarter than that and will retaliate pretty quickly. Your energy levels will drop and you'll actually be more likely to gain weight as your body will hold onto every calorie for as long as possible. The glow of your skin will also dim.

When I was younger and trying to tone up and get fit, I tried the method of skipping a meal by having a big lunch and no dinner. Worst decision ever! I had absolutely no energy in the morning for the gym. During my workout, I'd feel sick and as if I could faint when my heart rate increased. Even during the day, I'd feel weak and just 'off'. My body hated me for it and made sure to punish me. Thank god it did because it put me off skipping meals forever.

Smaller portions of healthy snacks and meals, comfortably spread throughout the day, is far more valuable than not eating at all. Find the foods you love and then embrace your appetite. I love it when I come back from a workout and I'm starving! It's a sign that I've kicked butt and I deserve something fresh and delicious.

When it comes to snacking, my go-to options are ... yummy dips. I always buy them from a health food store so I know they're not stuffed full of sugar and preservatives. Normally I'll have plain crackers and carrots with beetroot dip or sweet potato and cashew. Delish.

Another go-to snack of mine is boiled eggs. They're inexpensive, easy to prepare and jam-packed full of protein, which helps my muscles restore themselves after tough workouts. Eggs are a fantastically filling snack to have on hand.

If I'm on the run from job to job, meeting to meeting or in and out of airports, I always carry a raw protein bar in my bag, along with a banana and some raw chocolate. The raw chocolate is for the days I know I'm going to need a big boost of energy at some point.

Small, healthy snacks throughout the day will keep you energised and focused. They're absolutely vital for healthy bodies and busy lifestyles.

MY PANTRY IS STOCKED WITH ...

* Quinoa
* Brown rice
* Protein powder
* Cocoa
* Almonds
* Currants
* Pesto
* Vital-All-In-One
* Red wine vinegar
* Coconut oil
* Tahini
* Honey
* Apple cider vinegar
* Tomato sauce

No matter how old I get, I'll never give this up!

Fitness

Fitness is incredible. You know why? Fitness can add value to so many areas of your life. It can improve your mental health, your energy levels, your skin, your digestion and your sleeping patterns. Fitness can even help prevent injuries and illness. It's like magic.

To me, staying fit and active is non-negotiable because it's an essential part of my happiness. When I'm in shape, I feel balanced and focused. Aside from all its benefits, my best advice on fitness? Always be honest with yourself. If you know you can push yourself a little bit harder, do it. You'll reap the rewards if you do.

If I'm going to a HIIT training session, the hardest part of the session is anything that involves ... the rowing machine! It's a full-body cardio exercise that pushes me to my absolute limit in a short time frame. I have a love/hate relationship with the rower. When I am on it, I try to compete with the person sitting next to me. I literally feel as if I could throw up when I get off, so I have to take a breather afterwards. I love the feeling of a tough session though.

My favourite part of the workout involves ... boxing and weights. I love feeling that continuous burn the next day.

My favourite way to keep fit when I travel is ... a skipping rope. It's small and compact, so takes up barely any room in my bag, yet it's so powerful. Skipping gets my heart rate up in a short period of time. I can skip in the hotel room if there's space or outside. It's the easiest way to get a full-body workout wherever you are.

Sometimes you're exercising without even realising it because it's so fun!

People don't realise that surfing, wake boarding and water skiing have amazing effects on your ... butt muscles. Different sports activate different muscles — sometimes muscles you never thought you'd need for the activity. After a day on the water or behind the boat, you definitely feel it.

When I'm at home or outside without gym equipment I ... get creative. I look for things like a skateboard, benches, friends or nieces and nephews (people you can lift!), trees and balls. I use these things (and people) to focus on resistance training.

Fitness can add value to so many areas of your life.

If I'm suffering from cramps around that time of the month, my advice is to ... drink lots of water and tea made with hot water, fresh lemon and ginger. It's an easy and efficient home remedy. Also, give fish oil and vitamin B1 a go. Exercise is actually what helps the most, so I do my best to push through. Even if it's just a 15- or 20-minute walk around the block, this can help stretch and soothe painful cramps. Guys will never understand what we go through!

If I'm spending money somewhere in the fitness world, I invest in ... the correct style of shoe to match my workout. I do this because it's vital to protect my ankles, knees and back from strain and injury. You all know how much I love fashion, but when it comes to fitness, I'll choose support and fit over trends any day.

If I've been on holiday and I lose my general fitness and some strength, the best thing to get back to where I was is to ... start slow. I start by walking Isla to get my motivation back. Then I set the alarm and get up early for a gym session. Don't go too hard for the first couple of sessions back. Ease into it and remember to applaud yourself at the end.

Something I struggle with that I feel most people do easily is ... running. Despite being quite fit and strong, I've always found running tough. My body doesn't seem to cope with the impact. I must have the knees of a 70-year-old.

As I get older, the part of my body that needs the most discipline to stay toned and in shape is my ... hips. As soon as I let go or take time off working out, I see it in my hips. I get my hips from my mumma. Don't get me wrong, I love them as they give my body a womanly curve. However, I do like to make sure they stay toned.

Despite trends and popular brands, the most uncomfortable thing to wear during a workout is ... most types of undies because they constantly ride up my butt! I can't stand wearing undies that give me a wedgie every two seconds. I always wear a nude G at the gym.

My quick workout

Whenever possible, my standard workout is 30–60 minutes each day, ranging from cardio to weights and strengthening to long walks with Isla. I mix it up to make sure I'm working and challenging as many muscles as possible. Let's face it, though, sometimes life gets in the way and we need to get creative with our time and space. If my schedule is crazy busy, I have a series of go-to exercises that successfully gets my energy flowing, my muscles burning and my heart rate up. Even if it's only for 15–20 minutes, this is enough to get my body moving. Time limitations do not and will not define my health. The following can be done outside, in a gym or even in a hotel room. Combining a mix of these exercises will give you a tough, full-body workout — trust me!

Walking Isla is not only exercise, it's meditation as well.

Full sit-ups

I start with my legs straight up in the air and curl down into a banana shape. I see how many minutes I can get through, but never stop unless I feel the burn in my abs. A few reps do the trick.

Push-ups

Full-body push-ups are amazing for your whole body. I get as low as I can to the floor before coming back up. Ouch!

Leg raises

I do these on all fours. Good for my glutes.

Battle ropes

If I can get my hands on heavy battle ropes, I stand strong and swiftly move the ropes up and down to improve the strength of my abs, glutes and arms.

Planks

A few reps of planks can be a killer. I do both middle planks and side planks to get my obliques working.

Squat jumps or regular squats

These are great for activating my glutes. Squats are hard yakka, but the long-term gain is worth the short-term pain.

Mountain climbers

This is a great cardio exercise that gets my heart rate up.

Skipping

I always travel with a skipping rope. It's light to carry, gets my heart rate up super high and the movement activates my whole body.

Weights

Dumbbells, medicine balls and kettlebells are amazing for keeping lean. Women shouldn't shy away from weights for fear of developing bulging muscles! Weights are great for toning, burning calories (even after the workout is finished) and improving and maintaining the health of your bones.

If I can't dedicate a full 15–20 minutes to a workout before a shoot, I have a few tricks up my sleeve to ensure my body is activated and looking its best, which is important if I'm shooting swimwear or lingerie!

When I'm on set, before we get going I'll sit in the make-up chair in an ab hold (also known as a 'sitting hold'). It may look weird to everyone else in the room, but this doesn't faze me as I'm the one who has to strip down to a bikini with about 30 people watching! To do an ab hold, sit at the edge of a chair while squeezing your core in tightly for as long as you can. I don't move an inch to avoid interrupting the hair and make-up artists.

If there is enough spare time before we start shooting — such as while the production team tests the lighting — I try to squeeze in two reps of 20 full push-ups to activate my muscles. I might also do some leg raises while in a standing position; these are quick to activate my core and butt! At this point, I can't move around much as my hair and make-up is done and I've been fully styled, but moving around during the shoot is enough to keep my body energised.

Mindfulness and mental strength

These days our lives are so jam-packed — don't you think? We wake up and switch on, literally. It's almost as if the second our eyes open, our phones light up and we are ready and roaring. Pressure points and stressful situations follow us like shadows, so learning to cope or, better yet, find peace is imperative.

While it might seem difficult to completely switch off from time to time, it's not impossible. For the sake of your mindfulness (in other words, your ability to be present in the moment) and your mental health, you owe it to yourself to find time to rest and recharge. For me, this means investing time into eating consciously, staying active and listening to my body. Surrounding myself with positive, loving people and remaining a loyal friend are also incredible ways to nurture my mind.

The burst of endorphins I get after exercising each morning puts my mind at ease. It's one of the best feelings in the world. To get the most out of that rush, I know that my body needs at least ... 50 minutes of high-intensity training or a weights class each day during the week and a nice calm walk outdoors on the weekends.

During a workout, I know when I am giving it my all and I know when I'm slacking off. I bet you do, too. Keep in mind that the pain is short term. Sometimes it's just a matter of 15 or 30 seconds to go! I make myself hold onto every single second, knowing that if I don't, I'll feel annoyed or frustrated at the end. I know that my endorphin rush won't be as electrifying.

I try to stick to this routine as much as possible, but I'm the first to remind myself that it's perfectly fine to have a day or two off. I can feel it when my body needs a good rest, so I don't push myself over the limit. That's when injuries tend to happen. Plus, a bit of rest can help you gear up for an even stronger few weeks in the gym.

Even if it's not my body aching, there are times I get emotionally exhausted and sink into a negative rut. It's foul. To get my mojo back, I find sleep is king. I make sure to clock in a little more sleep (earlier nights and a few mornings away from the gym) until my sense of positivity restores itself. You can't drive a car without fuel in it.

I'm a huge advocate of getting enough sleep. If I'm feeling

To get my mojo back, I find sleep is king.

lethargic and my body is zapped of energy, a good night's sleep does wonders for my bones, muscles and mind. My friends sometimes call me a grandma because I love bed so much. It doesn't bother me, though, because I know I'm going to wake up feeling energised and ready to go every morning. Think of sleep like your iPhone charger. If you don't plug your phone in and allow it to recharge, it'll conk out soon enough.

In terms of my mental health and self-confidence, the age I found the most difficult was ... 14–16 because my body was changing. I felt pressure to look super slim at work and I was constantly comparing myself to others. At this age you lose a bit of control when it comes to your body because you're growing. As a woman, the shape of your natural silhouette changes. It's strange. But there's no point fighting it; you must embrace it instead.

I remember looking at top models wondering if I could ever look exactly the same as them. The answer was (and still is): no. I will never look exactly like anyone else, but I can still look and feel amazing in my own body shape and skin.

Around the age of 16 I changed my attitude and perspective. Moving forward, it was all going to be about maintaining a positive 'can do' attitude. This meant feeling positive towards my own body, and positive that I would make time to kick butt outside or in the gym to strengthen my body and increase my fitness from head to toe.

'Thin' isn't a word I use. My focus is on being strong and toned. With this in mind, I always remember that the less I eat, the less energy I'll have during a workout. I make absolutely sure to fill my belly up with goodness so I can smash out epic sessions every single time and leave feeling great.

Looking back, I've always received emotional support from ... my family. They've always been there to encourage me and give advice when I need a second opinion. During my teenage years, I also had a boyfriend who'd offer me his shoulder to cry on after a bad day.

Since meeting Josh, however, I feel a whole new sense of support and gratitude. Josh is more than just a boyfriend. He's my best bud and my partner. Josh has guided me in all kinds of

Activities like surfing or skating can be just as powerful as a gym session. You'll awaken completely different muscles ... muscles you never knew you had!

positive directions. He's always the first to remind me that my job isn't everything. When I am frustrated or impatient, Josh makes sure that I remember the old saying, 'If it's meant to be, it will be'. He also reinforces something I truly believe in, that 'everything happens for a reason'. Sometimes you have to trust the universe and relinquish control. I am lucky to have Josh as a calming influence. He subtly reminds me that my time will come; I just have to be patient.

When it comes to work, I used to be almost too loyal. I'd fly home from interstate or drive massive distances just to avoid causing the slightest disappointment. Looking back, coming all the way home from a family vacation for a two-hour job was probably not essential. I'd worry that a client might think negatively of me or write me off completely if I didn't go above and beyond.

I'll always do the right thing by my clients and be nothing but professional. However, it's also important (for your mind and your body) to live a balanced lifestyle. Keep in mind that this doesn't look the same for everyone, so avoid comparing your days to anyone else's. It's one of those things: when you nail it, you'll feel it.

Looking back, I wish I hadn't worried so much about ... other people in general and my hips. Now that I'm a little older, I've realised that things like this don't matter. My hips are my hips. Ain't nothing going to change them!

Feeling happy isn't always easy. It's normal to feel worried, sad, lonely or stressed. In these moments ... I turn to Josh for comfort and I remind myself that the feeling will pass. It might be one of those random 'off' days. It may be that time of month. Or it could be because I haven't been eating enough nutritious food (or have eaten too many Reese's Pieces!). Getting enough sleep, time to myself and exercise are all also important for me to feel happy.

During these moments or days, I need to find time to re-centre: switch off social media, get outside and prepare some healthy dinners for the week. I focus on freeing my brain of worry and recomposing myself.

When I notice my friends or people in my life are down or just not themselves, I always try to simply be there for them. I'll call them a few times throughout the day or week and check in to see how they're going or if they need anything. I always ask if they want to talk about what's bothering them or if they'd rather talk about something else to take their mind off it.

It's also nice to meet up in person if we can. If someone is hiding worry or pain, I can usually read it on their face and get a better idea of how best to support them. Going for a walk or finding somewhere private to chat are ways to help someone feel relaxed and safe.

Anger isn't something I feel often, but when I am feeling like I need to say something or stand up for myself, the way I handle it is to ... step away from the situation and ask for someone else's opinion first. This is so I can make sure I'm in the right before approaching someone. When I was younger I would bottle my feelings up to avoid speaking out. I would overthink a situation to the point where I'd explode in tears and frustration. Dealing with things in a calm manner is the best way to solve tension.

With maturity and experience, I've learnt to speak out when my gut is pushing me to do so. I've been walked over many times in this industry and — truth be told — I'm over it. I always do my best by everyone, so I simply expect the same in return, and so should you.

Small things that cheer me up include ... fresh flowers. I love having flowers in our home. They're beautiful and happy. I also burn fragrant candles, something soothing and not too overbearing.

Finally, a big fat cuddle from Isla and some quality time with Josh are the best cures. Finding one-on-one time with Josh can be tricky as we both have our own businesses and our schedules clash. But I love nothing more than squishing on the couch with Josh and Isla, no phones in hand and a delicious dinner is cooking away (with a healthy dessert to follow, of course). That is when I am at my happiest. It is pure heaven.

My daily mantra is ... work hard, play hard. It might sound corny, but this mantra fits seamlessly into my lifestyle and matches my personality. The harder I work, the more time I can book in for water skiing, skating and couch nights!

Body issues at a young age

As a young girl and a teenager, your body — not to mention your mood — goes through loads of changes. Let me ask you a question: did you or do you ever doubt yourself or feel negatively about your appearance?

I did. I used to compare myself to others all the time. I used to spot their perfections and compare them with my imperfections. There were days when I wished for a magic wand to swish around and change myself.

When I hit puberty, my hips grew a lot wider. After that, everything else seemed to get bigger and wider as well. To make matters worse, we all know that when our bodies change quickly, natural stretch marks occur. The keyword here is 'natural'. Stretch marks are natural and so common.

During the first few months of those big changes, I started to watch everything I put in my mouth in hopes of pausing the growth of my natural frame. Mum was quick to catch on to my changing attitude and started to reinforce the good old truths about health that we all seem to forget: healthy food and keeping active is all you need to worry about. If you do that with a smile on your face, you'll be fine. Mum was right. I embrace my body every day and treat it like a temple.

Don't get me wrong, sometimes we might feel a little down or flat for no other reason than that we're human. This is completely normal. Keep calm, keep healthy and keep that positive energy flowing. I swear, thinking positively can do wonders.

Q&A
MUSES & INSPIRATION

Mick Fanning

Three-time world champion surfer and
recipient of the Order of Australia medal in
2017, Mick Fanning is a champion in
and out of the water.

Q. You live a life of summer — a dream of Josh's and mine! Other than the surf, what is it about the coastal life that appeals to you?

A. Life is pretty great for me, yeah. For me, being around the ocean is calming and healing. I learn so much every day from being by the ocean — about the weather, animal behaviours and also people. It's a great place to learn.

Q. I've read that you're into Pilates and green smoothies. Have these been parts of your routine for a while now or are they new habits?

A. Ha, ha, I do love my green smoothies, that's for sure. As for Pilates, I got into it a couple of years ago. I was really into yoga throughout my career and thought Pilates was the next step. I enjoy how you get strength and flexibility out of it.

Q. You're in a very competitive line of work. How do you take time out for yourself and completely switch off?

A. When I was younger I couldn't switch off. I was competitive in everything. As I got older, I learnt that I needed to switch off, otherwise I would get too exhausted with it all. Now I can easily take a few days off and be lazy. If that's just sitting on the couch or exploring the countryside, it's all good to take a break.

Q. Any tricks or habits to get a good night's sleep before an important day?

A. I can sleep anywhere, any time. The main thing at night is to clear the head either by breathing or reading a book. Decompressing before you sleep really helps.

Q. How important is it for your mental strength to have a stable network?

A. Family and friends are key. People who are honest with you and also you can be honest with. Without these people, I would be nowhere.

Q. You're very generous with your time when it comes to charitable work. When did you realise how important it was to give back?

A. Thanks. Growing up my mum was a nurse so we learnt at an early age to give back. For me now it's about seeing kids smile. Even though we feel like we are giving the kids an experience, I get so much out of chatting and just seeing them smile.

Q. Your willpower and mental strength is world renowned. In a tough moment, what gets you through?

A. To be honest, tough and uncomfortable moments are when you learn the most about yourself. I always believe there's someone doing it a lot tougher than me, so I just suck it up and get on with life. It's not going to stop and wait for you.

117

CHAPTER
SIX

Beauty

Real beauty comes from within. There is no truer fact. If you feel happy, confident and comfortable in your skin, you will radiate. It might sound like a cliché, but it is amazing how a smile can completely change someone's face. All of a sudden that positive energy transforms the eyes and skin. They sparkle. To me, that's the essence of true beauty.

My honest advice around feeling beautiful is to treat your mind and your body with respect. Nurture the health and condition of your skin every day, stay fit and active and maintain a wholesome, balanced diet. If you get this combination right, from the moment you open your eyes in the morning you will feel beautiful in your most natural, stripped-back form.

Beauty isn't about covering yourself up with make-up; it's about being kind to yourself. Make-up is there to accentuate your features and complement a mood or an outfit. It's definitely not there to be a mask. I can't stand it when my foundation is caked on so thick that I can't even see my own skin! There are parts of me that might not be perfect, but I like them because they make me unlike anyone else. They make me unique.

I understand that sometimes we feel vulnerable or as if our spark of confidence has been momentarily smothered. These feelings are totally normal and only make us more human. Just ride the wave and let time bring you back to a place of peace. If it's one of those days today, let me share with you some of the tips and tricks I've picked up while modelling and simply while maturing as a woman myself.

By the way, I don't pretend to be an expert in beauty, health or fashion. Absolutely not. I am, however, an expert in the subject of 'sharing is caring'. One of my favourite things about women is our ability to create strong, trusted friendships without any secrets.

Real beauty comes from within.

Beauty notes

When I travel, I always carry ... moisturiser, a hydrating mist for long flights and car trips, lip balm and a CC cream. I apply the CC cream so that when I hop off the flight, I'm ready to put on my base colour.

Mints and treats are also must-haves. I always carry healthy goodies in case I get hungry on the plane. I'm also prone to sugar cravings. Making sure I can conquer the craving with something of substance is important.

Finally, I pack plain paper and a pen so I can doodle instead of sitting on technology for hours on end. It's a nice way to allow my mind to wander off. I find it keeps me calm and more rested.

I don't go to bed without ... having a shower and washing off my make-up. I apply a moisturiser or night-time oil to my face, as well as a hydrating lip balm. Josh insists we sleep with the fan on full blast, so my skin and lips get super dry. Hydration is key in my household.

For a healthy mind, I avoid looking at my phone right before bed. Night-time is when my eyes and brain are allowed to rest and completely switch off.

To keep my skin clear, my personal trick is ... regular peels. You wouldn't know it, but I've had troubled skin for years. I went through primary and high school pretty much unscathed, but when I turned

20 something changed overnight — for the worse. Like most teenagers I used to get the odd spot or blackhead from time to time, but when my twenties hit, those 'odd spots' turned into painful pimples that sat deep under my skin and took ages to heal. I tried so many products and skin treatments as well as regular peels, drinking loads of water and making sure my diet was clean and fresh, but nothing helped.

Just after I turned 24, my skin specialist recommended Roaccutane. It had become that bad. Obviously something as heavy as Roaccutane is a last-resort option. I was on a very low dose for about nine months. It gave me terrible headaches — so bad I could barely get off the couch. Eventually the headaches faded a little, but I felt tired all the time. Josh said I became 'moody' — a nice way of saying I'd become a grump!

I took the medication throughout *The Block* experience, which was tough to say the least. I kept it under wraps because I didn't want anyone feeling sorry for me. When the show wrapped, I was so proud of myself for getting through it, considering how tired I felt and how little sleep we got during filming. It shows how strong willpower can be if you're committed to something.

My skin has since healed, thank heavens! To keep it clear and fresh, I have regular peels. The peels help get rid of dead skin and hidden blackheads. (Those little ratbags are so good at hiding.) I use products that have been formulated by biochemists and pharmacologists as they show the best results.

In terms of investing money into beauty, I spend the most on ... foundation. In my line of work, I need a foundation that is hydrating and has long-lasting coverage. I also invest in good-quality skincare products, such as serums and moisturisers with SPF. I spend the least on eyeliner, lip balm, brow pencils and mascara. Price doesn't always equate to quality.

My beauty inspiration is ... Elle Macpherson, without a doubt. Elle's mind, skin and body glow with positivity and happiness.

The best way to go from a day look to an evening look when you only have 10 minutes is to ... darken the eyes with shades of rustic browns and enhance the overall look with a coat of mascara. Black eyeliner is also great to keep on hand as you can smoothly smudge it on your eyelid for a smoky effect.

The best trick I've learnt from a professional make-up artist is ... to let your natural skin shine through. Your make-up shouldn't be so heavy that it covers up freckles or anything else unique to your skin. You want your skin to look naturally enhanced, not hidden behind a caked-on layer of make-up.

In terms of my skin, the worst thing for me to eat or drink is ... sugar. If I eat too much sugar, I can see the effects on my skin the very next day. No joke! Also, if I drink alcohol I notice how dry and flat my skin becomes, so I steer clear of it. Self control does wonders for your skin.

The best trick for keeping your hair strong and thick is ... avoiding frequent colouring (especially for blondes). These days I only colour my hair twice a year and I ask my hairdresser to avoid taking the colour to my roots. I prefer it when I can see a little of the natural colour coming through.

The best beauty advice Mum ever gave me is ... to look after my teeth. Regular dental appointments keep them clean and in check. People often comment on the whiteness of my teeth and I have Mum to thank for that!

Celebrate your unique look

In grade 5 I had white blonde hair and the thickest, darkest, bushiest eyebrows. It was like having two fat caterpillars on my face, right over my eyes! The contrast between my blonde hair and dark brows was pretty significant and it stood out — big time. One boy in my class started to do what lots of little kids tend to do at this age: he made fun of my physical appearance. This kid went around telling everyone, 'Elyse has an ugly monobrow!' following it up with a big laugh and a cruel point of his finger in my direction.

Being young and vulnerable, I felt as though I was an alien from

Women need to replace the word 'different' with 'special'.

outer space because my eyebrows didn't 'match' those of the other girls in my class. I felt embarrassed and ugly. I went home, found Mum's tweezers and started plucking — not only my brows, but everywhere! Hair under my arms, my bikini line, my legs, my tummy, anywhere —I plucked it all out because that little ratbag made me think it was gross.

I went to school the next day, and for weeks after that, with the world's thinnest eyebrows and four stinging limbs. Worst of all, I felt self-conscious and embarrassed for being myself. Women need to replace the word 'different' with 'special'.

It wasn't until one of my first modelling jobs, when I was sitting in the make-up chair, that the make-up artist gave me a strange look. 'Elyse, what have you done to your eyebrows?' she asked. I told her that I was trying to keep them really thin, the way they should be. She gasped and replied, 'Honey! Thick, bushy eyebrows are in. You're so lucky to have them.' Her warm smile made me feel comfortable and almost embarrassed for not knowing this. She firmly advised me that I should stop plucking in case they never grew back. She was the pro, so I inhaled her information as if it was air.

To this day, I barely touch my eyebrows. I let them grow free and wild! I do tidy up the little area between my eyes, but have grown to befriend my bushy, crazy brows because they make me unique. Colourwise, the contrast against my light blonde hair is something I now enhance by darkening them with a pencil or powder. I'm even looking for a product to increase their thickness because I have learned to embrace the old saying, 'If you've got it, flaunt it'!

I also solved my plucking addiction by plucking my underarm hair instead. Now this is hair I am certain I do not want. If it doesn't grow back, good riddance.

It's no secret by now that despite my love of modelling and working in front of the camera, I feel the most beautiful and comfortable when I am au naturel — in other words, when my face is naked and totally make-up free. As I get older, this becomes more and more true. This may sound odd, because usually youthful, plump skin is what everyone tries to hold on to. However, as each year goes by I become more at peace with who I am and more aware of how to best maintain what I have.

The feeling of strengthening self-acceptance has done wonders for my confidence. Funnily enough, it's also helped the health of my skin. Worrying less about my appearance has reduced my stress levels and helped me fight off those dark circles that hang out under my eyes from time to time. Feeling good about myself allows me to sink into deeper and better sleeping patterns, which is heaven on a stick!

We all know that some women are blessed with gorgeous dimples, cute beauty spots, amazingly curly lashes, perfectly placed freckles and flawless skin. To you, some women might seem absolutely perfect in a physical sense. Let me remind you of something, though. These very same women might be looking at you thinking the same thing. Remember, women are not designed to 'match'. We are all different and distinctive. Celebrate the fact that you have something that is yours and only yours. And celebrate your buddy for having something that is only hers.

As they say, beauty is in the eye of the beholder. If you maintain a confident, generous and kind demeanour, your beauty will catch people's eyes in an instant.

The feeling of strengthening self-acceptance has done wonders for my confidence.

Create a solid 'beauty foundation'

I do, of course, understand that there are days when you wake up feeling flat or a tad drab. I know this feeling. After late-night flights, long days of shooting and very little sleep, waking up to a shrill alarm clock knowing that I have to jump in front of the camera again can be daunting, to say the least. If the day ahead consists of face-to-face meetings with clients and my game or my self-confidence is even one percent off, my motivation levels drop.

My new aim is to prevent these types of days from occurring before I wake up, or at least make them less frequent. To do this, I thought about days when I have woken up feeling like a thousand bucks, oozing confidence and smiles. On these days:

* my energy levels are roaring and I'm super keen to get up and get active
* my skin feels hydrated, smooth and nourished
* my eyes are free of dark, puffy circles and free of redness around the whites of my eyes
* my tummy isn't bloated, but instead feels hungry and excited for a yummy breakfast.

Now the trick is to work backwards from these goals. Every day I keep in mind ways to make absolutely sure that when that alarm goes off tomorrow I will wake up:

* energised
* radiant
* fresh
* keen for some tucker!

In other words, I've started to create a solid 'beauty foundation' right from the minute I get out of bed to the moment my head hits the pillow. My intention is to harness beauty from the inside out. Think of it this way: consider your face as a piece of art. Like all great artists, make sure you have a fresh blank canvas before painting your magic.

For example, to make sure I wake up with a settled tummy free from bloating and cramping, I put two things into my body every day: water (lots and lots of it) and apple cider vinegar. I add a few teaspoons of apple cider into my water bottle and sip it throughout the day. The water hydrates my body and rids it of any toxins hovering around, while the vinegar contains a heap of raw enzymes and good bacteria. Both the enzymes and good bacteria will help your body absorb maximum nutrients as well as kick-start the digestive system.

When my digestive system is happily churning along, I have great sleep, reduced stress and I feel light and energetic instead of full and lethargic. In other words, my 'canvas' is fresh.

Note that when I talk about beauty, I'm not only referring to my face. I consider my entire body and how I feel both mentally and physically. In my eyes, a beautiful body is one that is strong, energised and toned.

Keeping active is a huge part of my day, every single day. After a walk, a skate, a surf or a gym session, my face glows with satisfaction and pride. My smile gets bigger, my eyes come alive and I feel on top of the world. If this isn't real beauty, I don't know what is.

Skin

As I mentioned above, drinking loads of water helps keep my skin hydrated. When I turned 20, my hormones started to go nuts and my skin became prone to breakouts. If you are in the same boat, or you have been in the past, you know how distressing it can be — especially if it gets out of control. Before taking on any of my daily tips over the page, if you're struggling, I recommend visiting a dermatologist. They can help you understand what's causing the blemishes and irritations and you'll learn how to best prevent and cure them.

When it comes to maintaining smooth, nourished and plump skin, I stick to the following daily rituals. They are all super easy to adopt and maintain.

1 No matter how tired I am or how late it is, I wash my face thoroughly at night.

I start by removing my make-up, then hop in the shower to wash my face with a thick foam cleanser. (I always go with a foam cleanser over one with added microbeads as the beads can have harmful effects on the environment.) Next up, I use a natural walnut and oak cleanser to nourish my skin and leave it feeling silky and smooth. Last but not least, before jumping into bed I apply a moisturising night-time oil to give my skin a hit of hydration overnight.

In the morning my routine is quick and efficient. I apply a toning serum, followed by a moisturiser with SPF (SPF30 at a minimum). If I'm heading out, I then apply make-up.

The regime above might sound like a bit of an effort, but it only takes a few minutes and does wonders for my skin. I highly recommend finding time to do the same so you wake up feeling fresh-faced.

2 If I'm going outdoors, I am slip, slop, slapping.

Living in Australia means living under one pretty hot fireball: the sun. The UV rays here are intensely strong and while freckles might seem cute, they can become dangerous if you don't protect them. You also want to avoid sun spots, sunburn and wrinkles. The easiest way to ensure I am protected all year round is to use a daily moisturiser with added SPF (30+ is best). Find a light sunscreen to pop on under your make-up or a hydrating tinted moisturiser with added SPF. And don't stop with your face. If your body is exposed, get creaming!

3 I invest in a good face serum or moisturiser (with SPF) for everyday use.

As I travel so often and have a full face of make-up applied whenever I shoot, my skin cops a bit of a beating. Everyone has a different skin type, so if you find your skin to be oily, dry or you're prone to blemishes and breakouts, do some research before making a purchase.

4 I apply a primer before my foundation.

This is to prevent my pores from becoming too full of make-up. Primer can also add a touch of dewiness to the appearance of my skin.

5 I fill up on foods that contain skin-strengthening omega-3 fatty acids.

Salmon, walnuts, chia, avocados and pepitas are some of my favourites. These types of foods keep your skin looking plump and well nourished.

6 When I wake, I make a healthy concoction to nourish my body from the inside out.

Each morning I drink hot water with apple cider vinegar or lemon (or both). The vinegar is for gut health and lemon is for my skin. Lemon is packed with vitamin C, which helps even out skin tones and improve hydration. Vitamin C also contains a natural healing agent, which assists in clearing up blemishes. On top of this, the vitamin C found in a lemon helps reduce inflammation, meaning adios puffy, tired morning eyes. Who knew that sour old lemon could be such a great beauty trick?

Vital-All-In-One is a constant in my morning routine. No matter where I am in the world, this green goodness comes with me. Packed with prebiotics, probiotics, digestive enzymes, minerals, vitamins and more, adding 2 teaspoons to my smoothie or a glass of chilled water keeps my body feeling balanced and energised.

Lastly, I've recently come across a magic potion called Fire Tonic. Fire Tonic is loaded with ingredients such as horseradish, garlic, lemon, ginger, Szechuan pepper, thyme, parsley, rosemary and a lot more. I have a sip in the morning, which gives me an instant 'zing' feeling. My immune system feels well looked after too.

When I turned 25, I started dabbling in peel appointments, which I've grown to love. They help eliminate fine lines and bring hiding imperfections to the surface so they're no longer stuck under the skin. Peel treatments make my skin a little red the next day. It can take up to five days for my skin to calm down and return to normal.

Hair and make-up

Now that I've told you how I try to maintain a 'beauty foundation', let's move onto the more glamorous side: hair and make-up.

Foundation and concealer

I always use foundation that's suited to my skin type. Avoid thinking about the brand and instead go for ingredients to prevent breakouts. I'm in the habit of carrying two concealers: one for summer and one for winter. As well as covering blemishes, I use it under my eyes if I feel under the weather.

Cheekbones

I add an even sweep of bronzer under my cheekbones to create a nice clean contour. Quick tip: always tap or blow your brush before it hits the skin to make sure the bronzed colour isn't too strong in contrast to the tone of your skin. I also use highlighters

and illuminisers to add some extra light and moisture to the appearance of my skin.

If I'm using blush to create a rosy cheek, I only add a faint touch with a larger brush. You can get amazing creams and stains that are super easy to blend in, avoiding harsh blush lines.

Eyes

I'm all about 'less is more' when it comes to eye make-up. Make them pop, sure, but if you're going heavy on the eyes, reduce the intensity of your lips (and vice versa).

I love a thick, curly eyelash to feel glamorous and feminine. Paint your lashes on the top and bottom. A soft sweep of eye

shadow in a shade that makes the colour of your eyes pop is a must. My eyes are very blue, so I mix a few shades of matte brown, terracotta and orange to create contrast.

For special events, I'll add a few single lash extensions. I never use a full set as they're too heavy for me. Adding just a couple in the right places adds a touch of glamour to my look.

In my make-up bag, I always carry cotton tips. They are life-savers when it comes to fixing mishaps (like when you sneeze the second after you've applied mascara!) and help create clean lines if I'm using eyeliner.

Eyebrows

My brows are where I like to go wild! I spend the most amount of time on these bad boys and I love doing them. Saying this, I don't necessarily change them. I enhance their wildness by giving them a coat of colour and then brush them so they look as thick as possible. To colour my brows, I use a dark

brown powder and a short, dense brow brush or a brow liquid to tint the hair. Using a liquid also means you can spend less time at the beautician getting brow tints.

When I'm flicking through magazines, my favourite editorial look is when someone has insanely thick eyebrows that stick up. I adore bold brows. I rarely touch my eyebrows now. I pluck the random strays, and that's about it.

Lips

Keeping my lips hydrated is as important as doing it for my skin. As well as keeping a water bottle in my bag at all times, I always carry a fragrance-free, natural balm. The fragrance-free and natural qualities are essential, otherwise my lips become even drier.

When it comes to lipsticks and creams, I tend to go for nude colours because I like the softer finish. If I'm going straight from work to an event, my favourite way to add glitz to my look is to use a strong, bright-red lipstick.

Make-up is about accentuating your natural features.

WHAT'S IN MY MAKE-UP BAG

❋ Mascara

❋ Foundation

❋ Eye shadows

❋ Brown eyeliner

❋ Bronzer

❋ Highlighter

❋ Concealer

❋ Blush

❋ Lipstick

❋ Eyebrow serum

❋ CC cream with SPF

❋ Moisturiser with SPF

❋ Toner serum

❋ Night-time oil

❋ Eyelash curler

❋ A range of brushes

Hair

My hair lives a very rough existence. Working as a model means it regularly gets smashed. Hairdryers, curling tongs, straighteners, gels, sprays, serums and constant brushing this way and that way — it's brutal to even think about what I put it through. Josh and I also live active and outdoorsy lives. My hair gets a whole heap of sunshine and salt from the ocean, both of which can be really quite drying.

Very few clients (if any!) will book models with unhealthy, dry hair that is on the verge of snapping off, so it's vital to keep my hair in good condition. Plus, like any professional in any industry, I like to be known for professionalism and reliability. Making sure my clients can trust that I'll rock up in tip-top shape is important to me.

To keep my hair as healthy as possible, I book regular trims to get rid of split ends. Regular trims also encourage my hair to grow and keep it looking lush and nourished.

I also always have a leave-in hair serum ready to go. This adds so much moisture back into my hair and makes it smooth and shiny. Once a week, I pop a treatment on my hair overnight. Coconut oil can work a treat if you're not wanting to spend a fortune. I apply a lot of it throughout my hair before bed and wash it out in the morning. When it's dry the next morning, it feels like a brand-new head of hair. And it smells deliciously yummy, too. I also use the coconut oil on my skin as a deep moisturiser and when I'm cooking. Basically, I always have a jar of coconut oil on the go.

Beauty is personal to each individual. Each of us has things about ourselves that we love and things we have trouble loving. Just remember that the entirety of you is what is special. If it wasn't for those little unique and distinct features, you wouldn't be the same person.

BEAUTY IS PERSONAL TO EACH INDIVIDUAL.

CHAPTER SEVEN

Fashion & Style

Fashion has been a pretty big part of my life since the day I started modelling. It's an amazing aspect of my career because it constantly introduces me to incredibly talented and innovative people. Designers and stylists have a creative flair like no others. Their ability to visualise a look, a range, a shoot, a show is insane! Aside from the work aspect, I love fashion because it's personal to every individual. It's always changing and it is so open to interpretation. Fashion can be whatever you want it to be. Remember that the next time you're shopping or getting dressed for the day. Dress for you – for no one else but you.

There are so many aspects of fashion in my world. From my own style to working with a stylist or designer on a shoot, to launching my own label. I'm constantly learning new things and getting more involved in as many parts of fashion as possible. It's an industry I hope to work in for years to come.

My personal style

Getting changed in the morning usually begins with me rolling out of bed before the sun comes up, getting my hair off my face and slipping into workout gear: shorts, a loose singlet, a comfy sports bra and a hoodie if it's cold. Does that sound familiar to anyone? It doesn't sound all that glamorous, does it? Trust me, it's not. Despite the lack of glamour at this early hour, however, a day that begins with a good sweaty workout is bound to be a good day.

When my workout is done, I come home feeling proud of myself and great about the day ahead. My energy levels are bubbling away and my self-confidence is at its strongest because it's before 8 am and I've already ticked off a goal for the day. In my opinion, this is the perfect way to start your morning. Feeling positive in your own skin will make you excited about putting something on that accentuates your strength and your happy mood. You know it's going to be a good day when you step out absolutely owning your outfit.

Fashion should always be a positive area of your life, a fun outlet for being creative and personal. Fashion shouldn't intimidate you or make you feel negative in any way, especially about your body. If it ever does, whatever garment or trend you're leaning towards might not be the one for you, which is totally fine. There are particular cuts, shapes and styles that I don't wear because they don't do anything positive for my self-confidence.

When I'm not working, I avoid wearing things that bring annoyance or worry. Who wants to be pulling things up or down all day or worrying about undies flashing or straps falling down? Not me. Even if it's the latest trend in *Vogue*, if it's not easy to wear, it's not living in my wardrobe. If there is a current 'trend' going round, however, that you're keen to explore; make the trend fit in with your personality and your style, not the other way around. Make it your own. Fashion is one of the rare areas of life that has pretty much zero rules. You have free rein, so run wild!

Put it this way: if something you put on makes you feel uncomfortable, if something makes you feel negative about your body or anything less than beautiful, don't buy it. Go with the styles that accentuate your uniqueness and your personality. And go for comfort over labels.

My personal style in
a nutshell: classic,
simple and comfortable.
I love getting all
dressed up, but after
an hour I'm craving a
T-shirt and jeans.

Oh, and I love my sunglasses.

My style reflects my personality and my lifestyle. I like it this way because I never feel as though I'm pretending to be something I'm not; I always feel like myself. It's far too exhausting hiding behind a façade just because the magazines say we should. No thanks. I have more important things to focus on and I have no doubt that you do, too.

You'll notice that it's quite rare to see me wearing things that are overly constricting or make me look all swallowed up. I like to live my day comfortably. I usually have a go, go, go schedule, so it's important that I can move quickly and freely. Layers are good for me. Layering also helps me take a casual look to a slightly more sophisticated look in a matter of moments. Plus, it means I can warm up or cool down instantly, which helps enormously on my busy days.

From my Instagram you can probably tell that I'm a casual and classic kind of girl. For me, less is always more. Denim shorts or jeans are failproof, paired with a simple singlet or T-shirt and footwear that I can preferably slide into. Oh, and I love my sunglasses. My collection is getting bigger by the day. They're a great accessory to use when freshening up an outfit. They can change your whole look — and there are millions of styles to choose from.

If I'm concerned about the weather (which is a common and constant worry living in Melbourne!), I'll pop a shirt or jacket around my waist or on my shoulders. A warm, lightweight jacket or coat is a great investment piece, especially if you're someone who travels a lot. And the best way to add extra warmth to an outfit? Add a cute hat or a beanie. If you've been following me for a while, you'll have noticed that Josh and I love our beanies. They're great for bad hair days, too — an added bonus.

That's my personal style in a nutshell:
Classic, simple and comfortable.

Simple doesn't mean boring

Bear in mind that 'simple' doesn't have to mean 'boring'. You can quickly mix up simple basics with other textures, patterns and layers. When I'm feeling girly and summery, I like to mix whites or denims with a floral print or pastel shades — anything with a pop of colour. On days when I have back-to-back appointments and I'm constantly on the go, I stick with a monochrome palate: crispy whites, blacks, greys and, of course, a little bit of denim. This combination makes me feel slightly more sophisticated and professional. If I'm going for a snug and cosy look, I like knits and jackets with an earthy, rustic look. As with make-up, I go for tones that complement my colouring and don't wash me out. Matching your eye colour to a garment is always fun. It makes your eyes pop!

Then, of course, there are days when I'm as happy as Larry to slip into some old, ripped denim shorts, a rock'n'roll T-shirt and a pair of trusty kicks. Absolutely zero fuss. My favourite.

As I've said, I dress to suit my mood and my day. If someone takes a sneaky photo of me and my outfit ends up online or in a magazine, well, people are going to get what they get. When I'm not working, I dress for me and only me. I urge you to do the same. Forget about what anyone else thinks. Be comfortable and you'll ooze confidence and style.

Exploring fashion

I was introduced to the world of fashion at a young age. Mum would make clothes from scratch for Brayden, Tahlea and me. Impressive, right? Anything from shorts and shirts for Brayden to skirts and dresses for Tahlea and me — with matching little hats of course! With three growing kids, it was much easier for Mum and far more cost effective to take the DIY approach. Luckily for her, sewing was her hobby. It was win-win for our household.

When Mum stayed with me for that month in Hong Kong, it was the same year as my debutante ball (like a high school formal, deb balls are big in Melbourne where I'm from). While overseas, we shopped around looking for the perfect fabric to make my deb dress. Once we found it, we decided on the style and Mum very cleverly whipped it up. It turned out to be everything I wanted and

more. It was perfect: the right fit, the right style and we saved a small fortune. I grew to love and admire Mum's innovation, and I still do. She taught me that money doesn't reflect style. Style comes with a good eye, creativity and, of course, self-confidence. Fashion continues to be something Mum and I share. In fact, she recently made one of my headpieces for Spring Racing. I adored it because I knew no one else at the carnival would have anything similar. It was custom made, by the very amazing Mumma Knowles!

I grew up learning to love a good bargain; spotting a bargain from a mile away is one of my skills. At school I was pretty quick to realise that staying up with the trends had nothing to do with shopping at certain stores and buying particular brand names. We didn't have a uniform at my high school so it meant picking out an outfit every day. As long as I could comfortably run around, I wasn't fazed by the names on my clothing labels. Not giving into the 'brand hype' that always seems to exist in high school allowed me to save up for bigger, longer-lasting things — like my own car.

These days, I'm fortunate to have the opportunity to work with a bunch of different designers, helping them showcase their new ranges each season. I love this part of my job because I get

It's incredible h[ow] things can cha[nge] if you keep an open mind.

FASHION ITEMS I CAN'T LIVE WITHOUT

✳ Denim jacket

✳ Leather jacket

✳ Denim shorts and/or jeans (I still live in my Evrrydays!)

✳ Plain T-shirts and singlets

✳ Rocker T-shirt

✳ Blazer

✳ White collared shirt

✳ Coat in winter

✳ Big knit in winter

✳ Sneakers

to know the designers (and stylists) and learn from their brilliance and creativity. I learn about shapes, fits, mixing patterns with colours and textures. Most importantly, I've learnt to never judge something until I've at least tried it on. It's funny how quick we can all be to say 'no' to something on a hanger. That instant 'there is no way that's going to work on me' thought, which jumps into your mind after laying eyes on something for the first time. Since learning to leave my stubbornness at the door and trusting the experts, I have discovered so much about fashion and what suits me. It's incredible how things can change if you keep an open mind.

The best thing about fashion is that it's always changing and evolving. As much as I'll always keep my style on the laid-back side, I'm up for experimenting, too. What's the worst that can happen?

My final note on designer wear: don't feel too guilty about a splurge now and then, but saving should always be a priority. While you're still growing and exploring your shape and your personal style, do your best to avoid going overboard and spending all of your hard-earned money on clothes and shoes. As tough as it may feel, you'll thank yourself in the long run!

Dressing up

My job comes with quite a few events that require me to dress up and glam it up, such as fashion shows, the Spring Racing Carnival, store launches and the occasional charity dinner or ball. When an event comes with a red carpet, it's always a bit of extra fun.

My favourite red-carpet look of late was my outfit for the 2017 GQ Awards in Sydney, an ensemble styled by the dynamite Lana Wilkinson. I wore a one-shouldered gold mini dress with a floor-length flowing sleeve, high gold heels and slicked-back hair.

It was the perfect balance of sharp, chic and playful.

I feel pretty lucky when I have the opportunity to wear someone's incredible design. I get to momentarily step outside of my usual style and feel feminine and glamorous.

Getting dressed up usually means wearing a killer pair of heels. I have such a love/hate relationship with heels; I'm sure most women do. Wearing monster heels all day and all night can be the devil. I can honestly think back to so many occasions when it felt like my ankles were seconds away from snapping off my legs. Ouch! In 2015, I was the Rolex Grand Prix Ambassador. This was an absolutely amazing experience and I feel so privileged to have had the role but, holy moly, four solid days of walking around in the world's highest heels from dusk till dawn was challenging. I never let this kind of thing get in the way of work and professionalism, but I can assure you, I did not feel my toes for weeks afterward. I suppose, though, what doesn't kill you, makes you stronger! My feet are definitely made for Vans or runners. Actually, I think my feet are made to be left alone, free and barefoot.

If I'm headed to a formal event and will be on my feet for a long period of time, I always carry bandaids and those gel pads that go under the balls of your feet. They are a lifesaver. At the end of the day, heels look great. They make you feel long and tall and can make an outfit absolutely pop, but they also come with a fair share of painful baggage. On the bright side, at least your calves get a ripper workout.

I'm glad the flash wasn't any brighter!

It's nice to mark e occasion by doing mething special for yourself.

Splurging

If you've achieved something great — received a promotion at work or got amazing results at uni — it's nice to mark the occasion by doing something special for yourself. Fashion is one area of life where it's easy to splurge a little on the odd occasion to reward yourself.

Nowadays, I mainly splurge on homewares for Josh and me, but I still keep my eye on special fashion pieces from time to time. It must be a girl thing. The biggest present I've saved up to buy myself during my career has been a designer bag. The bag now marks a special point in my career. I'll have it for years to come and it will always represent hard work and commitment. The designer bag is green. I named her Avocado.

Before purchasing Avocado, I think the last time I'd splurged big time was right before I went to see Kylie Minogue with Mum and Dad. I was 10 years old and before going to the concert I went out and bought myself a new denim jacket. Obviously I wanted to look good for Kylie! Wearing that jacket, I had the best night ever. Since then, denim has become my wardrobe go-to. I live in it and I love it.

Josh's style

Josh isn't the keenest bean when it comes to shopping and fashion, which doesn't faze me, to be honest. I think Josh hits the shops about once or twice a year, maximum. I love the fact that he's comfortable and happy in a surfy, laid-back and relaxed look. It suits him and his personality. The two of us share a love for the surfy, street look. It's nice common ground.

I don't know if Josh notices, but I actually steal things from his wardrobe every now and again. I add his stuff to an outfit to finish it off and it always seems to work a treat. Thanks Joshy! When it comes to shopping with him or for him, I'm always happy to give my advice if he asks for it, but it's nice to see him wear whatever makes him feel completely himself. My main role is to make sure his clothes are clean and not covered in paint or holes!

When it comes to styling or dressing your partner, remember that everyone has feelings about what they do and don't feel comfortable wearing. Everyone has a certain style that is unique,

Wearing shorts
from my label,
Evrryday denim.

Everyone has a certain style that is unique, so let them roll with it.

so let them roll with it. It's important to let people be themselves. The alternative is to watch the discomfort on their face and in their body language and, let's face it, that is never a good look. Josh seems to be the happiest version of himself in a white T-shirt and jeans, which is pretty close to my own style, so it's fine by me.

Launching my own brand

During high school, I thrived in art and fashion. Any subject with a creative and hands-on approach was definitely a class where I shone. I learn so much more when I am able to do things, rather than read about them. We all learn in different ways, but for me personally, I'll take the practical approach over theory any old day. After I graduated high school I went on to study fashion and merchandising at Tafe. This style of education took me some time to get used to, but I stuck it out and absorbed as much as possible. I'm so thankful and proud of myself for that because a few years ago I used everything I'd learnt to launch my own brand, Evrryday.

I launched Evrryday in 2013, when I wanted a new challenge. I wanted to understand the different aspects of the fashion industry by getting involved with design, marketing and sales. And since I've always lived in denim shorts, I thought it was time to have a crack at getting my own pair on the market!

Launching a brand is tough. There is so much to think about and consider. I threw myself into the deep end from day one, managing everything from design to manufacturing, sales, marketing, customer service, packaging and e-commerce. I couldn't believe how long my to-do lists were each and every day. It's safe to say that my appreciation for everyone who works within the fashion industry has grown. It's a tough gig.

Managing Evrryday was an almighty task to take on while working full-time, but I loved the experience. My home and office at the time was our Coburg renovation site, so you can imagine the chaos! The house had virtually no walls and no floor. I spent hours hand-making labels and swing tags outside on the lawn and stacked the garments and packaging materials in any bare corner I could find. It was hectic, to say the least.

Having launched my own label, I now feel much more aware of

the industry I work in. There are roles and tasks I honestly never knew existed. When you get behind the scenes and see how much work, skill and passion goes into a fast-moving industry like fashion, it's hard not to be impressed. The speed of it alone was a shock to the system. Fashion is fast! There is no time for dragging your feet or umming and aahing. You need to be ready, alert, on the ball and confident in your decision-making skills. 'Chop, chop!' should be the fashion industry's slogan.

After I launched Evrryday, lots of people asked me, 'Why denim shorts?' I feel as though a comfy pair of denim shorts is a classic piece in all Australian wardrobes. I myself live in them. I never ever travel anywhere without at least one pair in my bag and I have no doubt they'll remain a staple forever.

When it came to the Evrryday range, I wanted to design a garment that was a durable, comfortable and stylish basic for everyday wear. Something that would appeal to all ages, shapes and sizes while fitting in with the active, outdoorsy lifestyle shared by so many Aussie girls.

You can run wild in these shorts. You can wear them down to the beach, out to brunch or dress them up at night with heels, a shirt and a jacket. The best part is that they're super easy to wash. Chuck them in a cold wash and hang them out to dry. Done.

As all women have their own shape and style, the shorts were designed to be worn in a variety of ways: high on your waist, low on your hips or even lower down to create a drop-crotch look. I have a pair in just about every size so I can style them to fit the day's activities. Versatility is pure gold when it comes to investing in your wardrobe.

Above all else, I wanted to design the perfect denim short that I personally loved. They were such a hit! Evrryday shorts were sold and delivered to girls and women around the globe. I hope that everyone who bought a pair will have them for a long, long time.

Above: Handmaking the leather labels on our back deck in Coburg (aka a building site!) Below: Josh helping out with the packing & posting.

Above all else, I wanted to design the perfect denim short that I personally loved. They were such a hit!

Handwriting thank you cards to go with each purchase – mid flight on a work trip!

Quick tip: The beauty of a basic Collecting basics is a great way to grow your wardrobe. You'll never go wrong with quality fabrics, neutral colours and classic shapes. I always have a few white T-shirts and one grey one in my wardrobe. Some are fitted, some looser, and all have different necklines. I dress them up if heading out and lounge around in them on days off. I'm always comfortable and not really at risk of looking 'dated'. A few pairs of jeans are another must! A slouched boyfriend pair and a more fitted jean with a higher waist are two good styles. This advice goes for shorts, too. We all know how I love my denim. If you can collect some simple bits and bobs in cotton, silk, linen and knit, you can mix and match your look till the cows come home. Statement pieces tend to date, but you'll never go out of style in a basic. Basics are definitely worth the investment.

THE KNOWLES FAMILY

Meet my sister, Tahlea

LET'S SEE WHAT THE YOUNGEST KNOWLES HAS TO SAY!

As Tahlea and I have grown older, our relationship has become stronger. When I was 18 and Tahlea was 14 we fought like cats and dogs! Now we are mates. We are there for each other no matter what.

Tahlea is a tomboy, like me. She is my ultimate.

All sisters fight. When Elyse is mad, how do you know? What are the signs of a bad mood coming on?
When Elyse is mad she doesn't talk much. She only wants to be with Isla. That's when you know! I've also noticed over the years that she definitely doesn't like to be asked questions when she's mad and she is the most grumpy when there is no food in the house.

Oh, and when I steal her clothes — look out everyone!

All jokes aside, what do you most cherish about the relationship you have with Elyse?
Despite her occasional icy reaction, stealing her clothes is probably what I cherish most. Some stuff just fits me better! But on a serious note, Elyse inspires me to be as determined, as hard working and as strong as she is. No matter how hard life gets, if you're passionate about something, she reminds me to never give up.

Can you summarise Elyse in a collection of words?
Bubbly, adventurous, a tomboy, a little moody at times and a dog whisperer.

Q&A
MUSES & INSPIRATION

Pip Edwards

Visionary and stylist extraordinaire,
Pip Edwards is the designer, co-founder and
creative director of one of Australia's leading
sports luxe brands, P.E Nation.

Q. You're a very inspiring woman, Pip. Where or from whom do you seek inspiration?

A. Inspiration is everywhere! I am perpetually inspired by every single thing, every single moment that happens around me. Art, music, fashion, friends, architecture, landscape, work, runway shows, conversations, meetings — there is inspiration everywhere!

Q. Since launching P.E Nation, what has surprised you the most in terms of what women want?

A. I knew there must be hundreds of women just like me and Claire [Tregoning, P.E Nation co-founder] and, basically, P.E was founded on what our own needs are.We are busy working mothers who want and need comfortable yet fashionable clothes to wear every day, but I guess we were surprised at how many women out there were in the same need! P.E Nation has escalated in such a short amount of time and that comes from the fact that we're delivering what our customer wants. We see ourselves as an active streetwear brand and that's what women want — comfort, fashion, flexibility and functionality all in one. They want to be able to wear their leggings all day, but not feel like they just walked out of a gym. They want to throw on an oversized jacket and know it works with jeans or workout wear. We launched P.E Nation because we selfishly couldn't find what we wanted, but it seems that that is what many others want, too.

It's so incredibly inspiring and humbling to know that we have resonated with so many other women.

Q. What is your favourite part about designing for the female shape?

A. P.E Nation certainly celebrates the female form, however we don't necessarily design for it — ha ha. Claire and I are tomboys at heart, so the fun with P.E Nation is that we don't have to create figure-hugging pieces to feel confident or even sexy. Confidence comes from the attitude and vibe. Obviously, our leggings are fitted and we use flattering fabrications and technologies to smooth and suck in the problem areas a lot of women have, but we also design really oversized pieces with a street feel for that rebellious edge, too. Women are such incredible beings — we are strong, powerful, multitasking wizards — so we love that we can design clothing that allows us to be all of these things and more, and feel great and look great while we're doing it.

Q. Is there something you once disliked about yourself but now love? If so, what led you to appreciate it?

A. I think every woman goes through periods of self-criticism. In fact, it can be on a daily basis. I'm lucky to be a pretty positive person, however, I'm of the motto, 'If there's something you don't like, change it!' Do something about it! I started Pilates about a year ago after an injury and was able to focus on my body and fine-tune it. I have noticed a significant difference in my shape and strength, not just in my body, but also in my mind. I am now tuning into my feminine grace, which I didn't acknowledge before, and I am loving that — the power that is behind the female form and the strength you find in your core. I learnt that I don't have to be hard to be strong and showing vulnerability isn't weak. Femininity is actually to have core strength with grace — to be strong from within, physically and emotionally. To openly be a woman, with that softness and nurturing care, but to know the power you have when you are in control of your mind and body. Pilates has allowed me to explore all this. And from this comes confidence. Confidence is feeling good within, feeling healthy, feeling fit, feeling balanced, which leads you to feeling happy.

Q. What do you feel women don't get enough credit for?

A. For being awesome! Seriously, it is so incredible to be part of a societal shift and this global momentum where women are given due credit, where women are supporting women, where all women are encouraged to shine. To see this rising feeling sweeping the globe is so infectious. I mean, there are some pretty incredible men/husbands/fathers/sons out there, too, of course, but times have

changed so much and women now have their time. We don't just have to be one thing — a mother or a businesswoman. We can be both, and so much more.

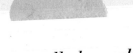

'I actually love what I do, every single day. That's what we should strive for. It's this feeling that creates success.'

—Pip Edwards

Q. I'm sure there have been some huge learning curves since running your own business. Can you share your top piece of business advice?

A. Trust. Your. Gut. Business has so many challenges that come with it and it's a constant juggling act between the micro and macro parts of the business. There are often many experienced voices sharing insights, but sometimes, when you are pushing boundaries and especially if it's your vision, you need to sit back, find some quiet and trust yourself, trust what you know, trust what you've learnt and believe it. You know your brand better than anyone else so find that voice and trust it.

Another piece of advice is to work out

what the big picture is for you. Really hone in on process and the mechanics of how a business works and understand the financials and your deliverables from the start. Train your mind to think business, not just creative. I was lucky that my trained commerce mind always made me think commercially. Commercial doesn't mean selling out, it just means that you are thinking in real terms of what's a viable business, given the landscape. And businesses operate to turn a profit. It's that simple. Today, I am lucky that I have found a sweet spot where my commercial training and my creative flair come together, almost in harmony. I am grateful for this every day. I actually love what I do, every single day. That's what we should strive for. It's this feeling that creates success.

Q. Apart from having your gorgeous little boy, what do you feel has been your greatest achievement to date?

A. My son Justice is definitely my greatest achievement, obviously, but I am so proud of P.E Nation, my second baby. Going from a conversation with a best friend to a global brand in two years is pretty amazing, but the greatest part of that is that Claire and I knew we could do it. We believed in the brand, in our vision and our point of difference, and we live and breathe it so that others believe it, too. This isn't just about selling product, it's a lifestyle and we are so proud of the 'nation' we have created.

Q. Health and fitness are big parts of your world. What is your favourite workout and why do you love it?

A. Pilates. I used to do a lot of high-intensity training and while I was fit and looked fit, I wasn't listening to what my body needed and what worked for my body. Pilates allows me to rehabilitate from the inside out and start a new fitness and health journey. It's all based around core strength, posture and softness and I'm addicted. I also do love a sweat sesh of boxing — it's always good to know what it's like to throw a punch!

Q. Describe your 21-year-old self in a handful of words, then describe yourself now in a handful of words.

A. 21 years old: Vanilla, innocent, unaware, disconnected and two-dimensional.

   Now: Interested, fit, has purpose, understands and acknowledges, real and motherly.

CHAPTER EIGHT

Staying Kind, Calm & Connected

Change can be scary. It always seems to come hand in hand with an element of risk. As you get older and your life begins to take shape, a whole bunch of new responsibilities start to rear their heads. Harder decisions have to be made, more expenses roll in and you're held more accountable for everything you do. And is it just me or does *everything* start to come with streams of paperwork, terms and conditions and the need to 'sign on the dotted line'? I loathe the dotted line! Adult life, hey, how spectacular ... not.

If you're anything like me, when you leave school, university or Tafe, you're filled with a sense of wanting to take on the world. You feel unshakable. When you're faced with 'the world', though, and reality sets in, it can feel slightly terrifying, Where's the map for the adult world?

Does the following train of thought ring a bell with anyone?

That job or that internship would be a great experience, but it means I won't be earning much. If I don't earn much, I won't be able to move out as rent will be too expensive. Oh! That reminds me, my car rego is due soon, too. When I'm working, where will I find the time to study? When will I travel? Where will I travel? How am I going to get up at 5:30 am for my gym class when it's 3 am and I am wide awake?

How is it that these crazy thoughts always seem to pop into your mind between 2 am and 4 am? Every day it's like clockwork.

If this is where you are at the moment, take my advice: take a deep breath and slow it down a few notches. Take life one step at a time because rushing won't do you any favours.

There is no textbook way to avoid feelings of stress and worry. We all have to learn to manage the feelings and cope in the moment. For me, fresh air, switching off my phone and exercise all help enormously. Most of the time I think it's our perspective we lose. If you can create a lifestyle and healthy habits that support you when you come across a bump in the road, you'll be fine. Here are some strategies I've picked up along the way to deal with the change and challenges of life.

Set goals

As I've said earlier in the book, lists are an amazing way to guide yourself. Writing down your goals and knowing what's important to you long-term will help you avoid stress about less important things. It can also help you make decisions when you're at a fork in the road. Lists of smaller goals can give a sense of purpose to your day and help you measure whether or not you're on track. You can't steer your ship without knowing where you want to end up. Things always take a little longer than anticipated, so don't beat yourself up if you're not ticking things off as quickly as you'd hoped. You'll get there.

To this day, Mum keeps everything I'm featured in. Whether it's a magazine cover, article or even just a newspaper clipping!

From the early days of my career, I wanted to tick off some pretty big things and I'm proud to say I've managed to succeed! Let me assure you, these successes came after a ton of commitment and a lot of hours doing the hard yards. The work was well worth it though because I've now managed to achieve the following:

* Become an ambassador for an admirable charity. Working with WaterAid Australia has been an eye-opening journey. I've met some incredibly inspiring people and visited some beautiful places. It's an honour working with their team.
* Book an ambassadorship role for an Australian sporting event ... the Rolex Grand Prix was an epic experience.
* Work with an iconic swimwear brand. My dream definitely came true when Seafolly invited me onboard.
* To land a magazine cover is a goal shared by many models. Having now worked with *Stellar* and *Women's Health* I feel very honoured.
* Get back into runway. Walking for Myer alongside Kris Smith was scary to begin with but so exciting!
* Book an international campaign — another major dream for many models. It takes persistence and guts, but if you stay focused, anything is possible.
* Explore a TV presenting opportunity. Working with *Postcards* on Channel 9 was an amazing experience. It took me out of my comfort zone initially, but I learnt so much and I had an absolute ball. I loved every minute of it.

And, of course, some personal goals:

* Buy or build a home with Josh.
* Launch my own brand (Evrryday).
* Maintain a lifestyle that champions happiness and health.
* Make time for myself to switch off and rejuvenate mentally and physically.
* Never succumb to industry or peer pressure.

My list of goals doesn't end here. There are plenty more bullet points to go and this list will keep on growing for years to come.

Life is a game of trial and error to begin with anyway. Your career path, where you want to live (at home? in a rental with friends? interstate? overseas?), travel plans and relationships. Personally, I always need to try a bunch of things and go about each of them a bunch of different ways before I find a rhythm that suits me and my lifestyle. For example, it took me a few years to find the right kind of workout for my body type and personality. I tried heaps of different types at various times of the day before I figured out what led to the best results and most suited my lifestyle.

Before jumping on a plane and moving to Los Angeles or Sydney to build my career, I visited both cities a number of times to develop a network and get to know the city. By investing so much time in each place, I've worked out that I can live comfortably in Melbourne while continuing to work away as well. I just need the right team by my side and good time management.

It's pretty amazing what you learn about yourself as you go. But we all have to start somewhere, especially when it comes to your career.

Stay true to yourself

Over the years I have worked with many agents and managers both here in Australia and overseas. While I have worked with some gems, I have also been disappointed. There have been times when I've had to call agents to ask why I wasn't put forward for particular jobs. I understand that I won't fit every job brief — but when I do, it's frustrating to not be given a fair shot. Hearing responses along the lines of, 'You don't have a story — the media won't be interested,' or 'You're not tall enough,' or 'You're too commercial and won't work for high-end jobs. You're only going to be an online model,' or 'Your social profile is not strong enough,' or, the very worst, 'Your relationship is not high profile enough,' can be really, really infuriating.

When people doubt me, it makes me feel undervalued and underestimated. I know what I can and cannot do. I've never relied on anything or anyone else to help me achieve something. I rely on my work ethic, my drive, my focus and my commitment. I've worked my butt off since I was 10 years old and I am here and willing to

Respecting yourself is the key.

give anything and everything a shot before ruling it out.

I've come to realise that when people underestimate you, it's your time to shine and prove them wrong. Hurdles like this are bound to pop up from time to time in our professional lives, so stay strong and true to yourself. Persevere and focus on the goal ahead even when you hit a rough patch. I feel as if a prerequisite for success is the ability and the willingness to 'keep on keeping on' regardless of the opinion of others.

Whatever career you choose, be smart and switched on from day one. Knuckle down and learn how things operate. People respect those who immerse themselves and show an eagerness to get involved. Look out for other types of roles you might aim for down the track and plan ways to get yourself there. Most importantly, use the time to work out who you want to be in the workplace. This will become clearer as you work with different people over time. You'll quickly discover who you'd like to be and who you'd like not to be.

From the beginning of my career, I've observed everyone and their manner. What stood out to me most was how they treated others. The people who were not only liked, but genuinely respected by the whole team — that's who I wanted to be. Surprisingly, that is a tough person to become. I had to grow a strong backbone early on. I had to be able to stand my ground and speak up when I would have preferred to crawl under the covers and ignore particular conversations and situations. Respecting yourself is the key. Like Pip said, you know in your gut what is right and wrong, so let that steer you. It will not fail you, I promise.

Right from the start I decided to remain loyal, kind, generous and be as involved as possible. I prioritised my integrity and surrounded myself with like-minded people. You can't always control who you work with — sometimes you can't even control who you hang out with socially — but you do always have the choice to not allow others to influence you.

I once was flown to Jamaica for a job. It was an athletic shoot for an American fitness magazine — a dream job for me! Well, at least I thought it was. I arrived at the shoot ready to introduce myself, meet the team, take directions and work hard despite the harsh 40-degree heat while styled in heels and a thick sports

No matter what's going on in my life, being outdoors or by the water makes me feel centred and calm.

jacket. Working in tough conditions like these is fairly normal for a model — you shoot winter looks in summer, and summer looks in winter, go figure! — so it didn't faze me too much. What did floor me, however, was the photographer's attitude. He yelled at me the whole time. 'Do this,' 'Do that,' 'You're doing this wrong,' 'Move faster,' 'Try harder'. This was not constructive criticism; this was obnoxious, unnecessary intimidation and it was breaking me down.

When the shoot was over, I took my shoes off and approached the photographer. In a calm, deep voice I told him to stop talking to me in such a manner. I turned around before he had a second to respond and walked away, trying to hold off my tears. He'd crushed my spirit, but I was not going to let him see. That day taught me that no matter who is on a shoot with me — the best stylist in the world or an 18-year-old intern — every single individual will have my full respect and gratitude from the minute we arrive to the minute we wrap up. We are all people and deserve to be treated with mutual respect. If it's not an environment where everyone feels happy and safe, it's not an environment I want to be in.

I work in fashion, beauty and in the media: industries that can all be harsh. I wake up to articles with my face all over them and not one word of truth to the story. Apparently, I've been married, engaged, pregnant — the lot! It's ridiculous. This frustrates me like nothing else, but I never give into it. I know who I am. I know the truth about my life and that's all that matters. Letting people influence you is too common among girls and women. We need to stick together and look out for one another. Women have a special universal bond, but it can sometimes get trampled by gossip and petty bitching. Choose not to get involved.

Find your tribe

As you get closer to your dream career and your dream lifestyle, take the time to look back and feel a sense of pride. Getting through the turbulent times along the way and walking through unknown territory is hard yakka, so giving yourself some credit is healthy. It's also good to surround yourself with people you love and who love you in return. The company you keep makes a significant difference to your day. Family and friends keep your heart beating

Friends who love me just the way I am — and the feeling is mutual!

The company you keep makes a significant difference to your day.

and the drive running through you. Don't let them out of your sight.

Another special part of growing up is extending your family to include the loving and supportive people you meet and befriend. A number of people I've met through work have become like best buds — photographers, stylists, other models. If you click with people and share the same values, your support network flourishes. Keep these people close and cherish them. They'll be your safety net if things get tough and you'll be theirs. Remember that a friendship should always be a two-way street. If it's not, be brave and say something or be at peace knowing that not all friendships were made to last. True friends should feel like your family.

These days, I am a good judge of character. I stay close to those who don't judge me or become envious over silly, trivial things. I'm fortunate to have the chance to visit amazing places and meet great people, however these opportunities haven't fallen into my lap. Some people forget the years of hard work I've poured into my career. Life is about positivity and joy. I surround myself with people who choose to support their friends, not critique them.

TRUE FRIENDS SHOULD FEEL LIKE YOUR FAMILY.

It should be easy to work out who your friends are. They're the people you can call at any time to vent, cry, chat, laugh or just talk about stupid things. You know when you are with someone but you're tired or engrossed in a book, so you sit comfortably in silence for hours? That's a true friend! When you're unafraid to just 'be', you're in good company.

I often get so tired at the end of the work week I can hardly hold a proper conversation. Thank god Josh is so patient. There are some weekends when I wake up wanting to hide away at home with Josh and Isla and switch off from the real world. Since filming *The Block*, especially, our personal lives seem to have caught the media's attention. We feel so lucky to have been on the show and we are grateful for the support we've received since it wrapped up, however the attention that followed can be exhausting.

Despite the recent media hype, however, Josh and I never let it come between us. We always make time for date night, when we enjoy each other's company and switch off. A date night for us can be as simple as walking down the street and trying out a new restaurant, but we love it. We use the time to talk about anything and everything. If we need to, we'll get things off our chest that we haven't had time to chat about during the week. Communication is key in a healthy relationship. We feel it's important to keep each other informed about everything going on in our respective lives. We're a team and we have each other's backs, no matter what.

Whenever Josh and I have the time, we love to escape the city for a weekend and go exploring. We adore our home but every so often it's good to get away. As we have spent years building and renovating, it becomes easy to slip into a routine of spending all day Saturday and Sunday painting, gardening or doing something else to the house. If my computer is set up, I find myself replying to emails and going into work mode. This is a danger zone!

Josh and I like to live a balanced lifestyle where we spend as much time outside as we do inside. We try hard to make time to get away — to the beach, the bush, wherever we can find space to relax. Josh is my best friend and one of my biggest sources of support. Where he is calm, I am crazy. Where he is measured, I am creative. I like that about us; our differences create our balance.

To end the note on friendships, let's go back to the idea of choice: choose happiness over popularity. I work in a world where it can be hard to distinguish who is genuine and truthful, who I can trust and who treats me as a real mate rather than an industry connection. I'm never swayed by those who shower me with compliments or promise me the world. I'm swayed by those who protect me, who offer their honest advice and who are simply there when I need their support.

You can't always control friendships, but you can control the type of friend you are. Choose to be a decent friend; they're the very best kind.

Our differences create our balance.

Ride the wave

As you go about your days, as your career takes turns, your goals chop and change and perhaps friendships change, too. Your world will become personal and distinctly your own. It gets better — and better! It may feel chaotic at times, so do your best to manage the chaos and stress by creating coping mechanisms. When I feel anxious or uneasy, my coping mechanisms are to switch off, go for a walk or get a huge dose of fresh air. I find the perspective I've momentarily lost and my confidence slowly returns. Remember, you can't control everything in life. The best thing you can do is embrace all the twists and turns, even the challenges. Your happiness will naturally take form if you champion friendships, self-respect, loyalty and kindness.

Over the course of my career, I've had to pick up and relocate for a few extended periods of time. As much as I'm driven to work hard, I always find it tough leaving my home and my family. In addition to Hong Kong, I went over to the United States at seventeen and then returned twice for a four-month stint and a six-month stint at ages twenty and twenty-four. I spent most of the time in Los Angeles, but I was constantly flying around to different locations (New York City, Las Vegas, Dallas, San Diego, Utah, San Francisco, Seattle, Minneapolis, and so on). The American market for models is great, but you need lots of energy and a thick skin. You're always told in this industry 'America will make your career!' but, let me assure you, nothing just 'happens'. As soon as you touch down on U.S. soil you must be prepared to work your butt off and deal with forceful personalities, high levels of competition, tough feedback and a lot of expenses. It's an emotional rollercoaster and a hefty financial investment. I don't mean to scare anyone off! I just think it's worth knowing the realities of the move before going there. I wish I'd been more mentally prepared prior to my first U.S. trip.

During my two longer stints I grew mentally stronger. While based in L.A. I worked crazy hours day after day, after day, after day. My agency scheduled little to no downtime and I was worn out. I'd be up at 4 am trying to squeeze in a workout in my room before jumping on a plane to travel to a shoot location or starting a day of e-commerce. (E-commerce is when models shoot for a brand's online stores. You're sort of like a mannequin for the day.) I'd be shooting 200 to 300 looks per day at times, which is gruelling to say the least. It might have been a tiny bit better if I'd had a comfortable living arrangement, but I was living out of cheap hotels (one night I came home to find another model sleeping in my bed!) and eating terrible food. My mind and body had no chance to take a breather. It was intense and I came close to breaking point. One surprising saving grace kept me going. After a super-long day working, I arrived back at my hotel to find a package from Joshy. He'd sent me a ring and engraved the words 'I love you' into it. Knowing he was supporting me from back home gave me an extra dose of determination.

During that same stint, after I'd been in L.A. for about five months by myself, Josh came all the way out to visit. But despite him coming out, I barely saw him. I was lucky to get a full day off to show him around. I started becoming distressed with exhaustion. Eventually, I'd had enough. Josh was off to travel around Mexico for a while so I decided to go with him. It was not that I was sick of working hard, nor was I giving up. I was listening to my body and respecting the fact that it needed a break.

As a model you must have the courage to put your own needs first when it really counts. While it's great to be busy working, if your mental or physical health is compromised in any way, you need to stand firm and speak up. Having these conversations with your managers and agents can be awkward, confronting and intimidating, but those who care about your welfare will understand. There is truth in the saying, 'Short-term pain for long-term gain'. Keep the big picture in mind. If you want your career to have longevity, you simply cannot afford to spread yourself too thin and wear yourself out too early on. It's just not worth it. So I ended up leaving L.A. and travelling with Josh knowing that I'd be back, fighting fit, in the not-so-distant future.

The thing about the U.S. is that one tough trip is usually just the first of many. Models should continue going back and forth to work, add to their experiences and portfolio and sustain healthy relationships with those who have been contributing to their careers. So despite knowing that the market was a tough one to crack and keep up with, I decided to return to L.A. four years later. This time, however, I was going in knowing what I needed to prioritise in order to stay strong and positive for as long as possible. I went with more of a game plan. I knew that I needed to stay in my own Airbnb in a safe and central location. I knew the type of work I needed to book to further my career and expand my portfolio. Most importantly, however, I knew that I had to go at a pace that was realistic and healthy.

Just making the change to my living situation made a huge difference to my mindset. I made more time for quality workouts, outdoor hikes and time with friends. Staying in West Hollywood meant that I could walk to healthy food spots and maintain a nutritious diet, which was great for my energy levels. I actually ended up walking everywhere: to work, to brekkie or dinner, to the gym. I was getting in about seventeen thousand steps per day! Having this new plan of attack from the start made the sacrifice of leaving my family behind more meaningful. I was there to further my career and my future, for nothing else.

This second L.A. stint felt a lot calmer. I was happy with how I handled the travel and my feelings towards the city had definitely warmed up. It's such a beautiful place, full of creativity, life and opportunity. You just need to see through the storm and focus on the sunset at the end of the day. So if you decide to make the trip over to the U.S. and live there for a period of time, give it your all but always remember: look after yourself.

Get excited about life.
You only get one, so make it a bloody ripper!

THE KNOWLES FAMILY

Meet my brother, Brayden

THE QUESTION IS: DO I TRUST MY BROTHER TO BE KIND

Brayden and I have an amazing bond. He is the ultimate Aussie bogan! I think his personality rubs off on me from time to time, which I love. From motorbike riding to building epic jumps for our bikes to making booby traps when we were kids. We always seem to have a guilty look on our faces.

Running wild is what we do best!

What is it about Elyse that makes you feel really proud of her?
There's nothing that makes me prouder of Elyse than when she is on the motorbike in the middle of the bush getting smashed with mud and absolutely loving it. Whenever we're at the bottom of a massive hill, Elyse looks up at the height and then looks back at me with a frightened face and I tell her, 'You'll be right!' When we get to the top, seeing her massive smile makes me proud of the fact that she's game to give absolutely anything a solid crack.

Okay, now hit us with the good stuff. What is it about Elyse that can drive you up the wall?
When she chooses a green smoothie over a round of beer pong.

Can you summarise Elyse in a collection of words?
Fun, happy, wild and loud!

CHAPTER
NINE

Home

Home is where the heart is. This couldn't be more true for me. I've always been a homebody at heart. As much as I love getting all frocked up for a special event or a shoot, nothing makes me happier than being barefoot, barefaced, dressed in shorts and a T-shirt and cuddled up with Josh and Isla on the couch at home. It doesn't matter if it's a Tuesday night or a Friday night, I cherish the privacy and comfort of our home. It's my haven.

Just tonight, for example, I came home from work, popped salmon in the oven, jumped on the couch and yelled out to Isla, 'Aaaah, you don't know how good it is to be home, honey!' Being within our own four walls makes me feel calm and tranquil – well, most of the time anyway. Josh and I have been moving and renovating a lot recently, meaning that a certain degree of that calm atmosphere is hidden beneath the hum of a power tool. On top of this, our living space is currently polluted with about a million exploding boxes waiting to be unpacked.

But despite all the noise, chaos and lists of things to do, there is simply nothing better than coming home.

Decorating your space

When it comes to your living space, dedicating time to create areas that feel warm and personal will make such a difference to the enjoyment you get out of your home. I love being at home because every room represents a little bit of Josh and me: our lifestyle, our family, our memories. We are all so busy these days. Everyone is always out and about and so actively connected and open online. But when it comes to your home — whether it's your room at your parents' place, a room in a share house or your own house or apartment — treat it as your private sanctuary: a place where you will feel at ease and completely relaxed.

Your priority is to create an area where you're totally free and switched off from the world beyond your front door.

I've lived in some old, run-down places, don't you worry! I know that overwhelming feeling of 'where do I even begin?' But it's absolutely possible if you think creatively and innovatively. If you are currently sitting in a room that feels a little flat, empty or soulless, turn the page for my go-to list of ways to spruce up a room or an entire house. Whether you are renting or you own your place, making it feel homely and personal will make such a difference to your comfort level when you are home sweet home.

My favourite quick and simple home makeover tips

Giving a space a fresh look doesn't always require a big budget. A little innovation can go a very long way.

1 Rearrange the furniture.
Moving furniture can make a huge difference! Even just shifting the angle of the couch can make a room look and feel completely different. Shuffle things around to create more openness and light and help the space feel inviting and balanced.

2 Paint.
If you own the place, a fresh lick of white paint on the walls does wonders.

3 Use mirrors.
Hanging a mirror or leaning one against a wall can help a small space feel bigger. You'll notice the difference in a heartbeat!

4 Pot a plant.
Fresh flowers can be expensive to buy every single week, so indoor plants are a fantastic alternative. They're cost-effective, easy to maintain and are a great way to add instant pops of life and colour.

5 Change the window treatments.
Replace old, dark and dusty curtains with something lightweight to allow more natural light in. An alternative to curtains is white shutters. They look super cute and make a home feel cosy and inviting.

6 Add small touches.

Magazines, lamps, baskets, books and candles are examples of things that don't cost a fortune but are guaranteed to add so much warmth. Artwork is pricey — but art is really anything you want it to be. Leaning your surfboard against the wall or popping your guitar in the corner can be your art! Things like this bring charm, character and personality into a room.

7 Hang your TV.

If it's an option, mount the TV on the wall instead of using a cabinet to instantly create more floor space.

8 Declutter.

Taking the time to get rid of unwanted clutter is essential! Remove any knick-knacks that you feel are just wasting space. Less is definitely more when it comes to interior styling.

9 Add cute pillows.

Placing some new pillows or a throw over the couch can completely change the look and feel of a room. This is also a far cheaper way to revamp the couch, rather than buying a new one.

10 Get out the mower.

Try your best to keep your outdoor area neat. Josh is obsessed with mowing our lawn. I must admit, a freshly cut lawn makes the house look amazing.

11 Clean up!

I always feel so much better when my home is clean and free of clutter, mess and stuff. If you spend fifteen to twenty minutes cleaning up every few days, the place will feel as good as new. Like mowing the lawn, vacuuming the carpet adds a sense of newness!

Adding your personal style

Josh and I have moved around a lot over the last couple of years, so we've become good at creating liveable and personable spaces wherever we're living — which these days, is usually a building site! Even if it's just one room or one little corner within a room, we try to find a space to keep clean and calm where we can sit and think straight for a second or two. Slowly, as the bones of the house take shape or as we start to unpack and the chaos settles, we get into styling mode. There's no point starting the styling process if there's still paint and dust everywhere, so patience is important here. Styling is my favourite part of the whole building/moving process, so when it's time to get going, I am all aboard.

Josh and I get out Instagram, magazines and Pinterest and we start chipping away at a mood board. There is nothing we recommend more than a mood board when you're designing your house. It keeps all of your ideas together in one place and allows you to visualise how things will look when they're placed together. Fabrics, wall colours, furniture, decorative items, lighting — the lot. A mood board will also help you refine the styles you like so you end up with consistency and flow throughout each room. Josh and I had mood boards all throughout *The Block* and let me tell you, they were lifesavers.

You can easily start a mood board by collecting a bunch of images online. Then create different folders on your desktop so you can sort and find them easily, saving each image into its relevant file (Bathroom, Kitchen, Living, etc). If you have the time and access to a printer, printing out images and pinning them onto a cork board is another great way to establish your interior styles and designs. On the board, you can add magazine clippings, articles and fabric samples as well. On top of all this, I tend to carry around a file of plastic sleeves full of photos, clippings, samples and so on. The file comes with me when I go shopping or to visit a contractor. I am a visual person, so I need a visual aid on me at all times to make sure I stay on track!

Creating moodboards takes me back to my arts days. I used to sit and scrapbook after school for years. There is nothing better than having books and boards you can hold and feel.

When it comes to styling our home, Josh and I always make sure that each room suits our needs and our lifestyle. There's no point having a stunning room to look at if you can't live in it! A house is meant for living. If everything is too polished, too neatly placed and too white, it's not going to be a realistic space. So, think rationally right from the start.

For Josh and me, we have to bear in mind that Melbourne is quite a cool place to live for a big chunk of the year. Creating a home that looks and feels warm, inviting and cosy is vital for us. We always, however, make sure the house can also be opened up in the summertime and made to feel spacious with natural light and fresh air streaming through. Big open windows, skylights and concertina doors are great ways to introduce an indoor/outdoor style of living to almost any house.

We like to stick with a natural colour palette when it comes to the main architectural elements and the bigger pieces of furniture. We add pops of colour, pattern and texture through the soft items, such as linen, towels and pillows. If ever we are unsure about a colour, we go with white, white, white. White is always a safe colour. You can never go wrong with white.

A final tip on the colour of the walls. Of course it's our personal style, but we'd really advise against getting overly excited about wallpaper. It's a difficult material to get right and is super tricky to get off. We avoid it altogether.

To me, home is about family. It's about the memories I'll make as well as the memories I have collected over the years. Little bits and pieces from both of our childhoods make appearances in particular rooms. I have a chest of drawers I adore and an old film camera that follows me from house to house. Funnily enough, Josh and I each have a chair given to us by our respective grandparents. Josh has the old rocking chair his mum used to feed him in and my nan, who was an artist, gave me the chair she used to sit in while painting. I cherish them both. They are two pieces of furniture that represent a part of our history.

A house is meant for living.

Renovating

To any new home owners who are in the middle of renovating or who plan to renovate, Josh and I have some advice: plan ahead! Have a Plan A, a Plan B and a Plan C. And have all the plans in place from the start. Having back-up options is absolutely vital because things don't always go to plan. Further to this, there are little hidden costs under every nook and cranny when it comes to building. I hate to sound like a gremlin, but trust me when I say that something will go wrong at some point, and something will cost more than you anticipated. It's best to be prepared, people! I cannot stress this enough (nor can Josh).

Josh and I have popped some of our most important renovating tips on the next page. Before you go ahead with anything, make sure to invest time into research. Knowledge is power.

When getting a quote, never go with the first one; get two, three or even four. Always get a second opinion. And think strategically and long term. There's a lot to be learnt and considered in the property market, so don't shy away from asking questions if anything confuses you or makes you uneasy. There is no such thing as a silly question.

Josh & Elyse's top renovating tips

* **Find an ugly duckling.** We generally look to buy one of the worst houses on the best streets in a blue-chip area: a diamond in the rough — or, as I call it, an 'ugly duckling'. Never underestimate what you can do with an older place.

* **Sit down and create a budget.** When you're doing this, make sure you're allowing yourself to live realistically and comfortably. Having said this, be prepared and willing to make sacrifices. Short-term pain for long-term gain!

* **Have a Plan C.** Always include a contingency plan or two for unexpected hurdles and costs.

* **Be realistic about costs.** Create a feasibility plan to ensure you stay within your means during the process. It's crucial to know and understand your budget relative to the costs involved. Research and planning ahead can save you thousands!

* **Secure reliable tradies.** Do some research and ask people you know and trust for advice or contacts.

* **Work long hours.** Committing your own time can save you a lot of money, allowing you to do a lot more than you would otherwise. Don't be scared to get your hands dirty!

* **Don't skimp on your finishing tradies.** This includes plasterers, painters, tilers and so on. After all the hard work, a cheap or dodgy finish isn't going to do you any favours.

* **Step outside the box and dare to be different.** Your home should be a reflection of you. Having said that, keep in mind that sometimes less is more. Simplified designs are less likely to date and more likely to appeal to a wider market if your goal is to sell.

* **Use unique materials.** If you're able to, incorporate eye-catching materials in a few areas of the house. Make particular things memorable and get people talking!

* **Research trends.** Forecast trends by doing some research online and talking to people in the industry. Sometimes you'll nail it and sometimes you won't. It's all a learning curve.

* **Invest in quality.** The cheapest option is not always the best option. Investing in quality from time to time is essential for longevity. Work hard and keep that savings account healthy.

* **Don't rush.** Quality is the top priority. Take your time to do things properly from start to finish.

If you are lucky enough to have two hands, use them!

Josh and I believe in hard work. Always do as much as you can before outsourcing work. It will save you money and create some great lasting memories.

THE KNOWLES FAMILY

A few words from Josh

MY PARTNER IN CRIME

There is no one in this world who I'd want to spend the rest of my life with other than Joshy. We've faced plenty of hurdles and always get through side-by-side. Love you always and forever.

Be honest: what is Elyse's worst habit?
Elyse's worst habit is undoubtedly her hoarding! She keeps everything, to the point where we have so many multiples of things that never get used.

Elyse tends to receive a lot of clothing from different designers. Her wardrobe is pretty out of control. Being the hoarder she is, Elyse cannot bring herself to get rid of anything, which is a slight issue as we're living in a small two-bedroom house that has no storage. The walls will be bursting at the seams pretty soon. I think this is what

we argue about most: all her stuff.

The habit of hoarding was definitely inherited from her mother, who has kept Elyse's baby teeth and the hair from her first haircut as souvenirs. Weird!

What does Elyse mean to you? Why is Elyse so special and unlike anyone else you've met before?
We started dating just over five years ago. The thing that made us gel from the start was the interests we shared. We love adventuring and being outdoors. We believe in hard work and focus on progressing our careers and achieving goals.

Elyse and I set new long-term and short-term goals at the beginning of each new year and then work pretty tirelessly to tick them off the list. To date, we've managed to accomplish some of our long-term goals in just three years, which is pretty epic considering the size of them. Even we're speechless looking back to see how far we've come. Elyse is a motivated individual. She continues to strive for success, even during the times where she's pushed to the point of exhaustion. She shakes it off, picks herself up again and off she goes.

She's also a very loving, caring, selfless and grounded individual, who will just do anything to make sure everyone is happy and feels comfortable.

Without a doubt, Elyse is the only girl I know who could have completed *The Block* up to a professional standard. During the build, she'd continuously ask questions about what we were doing, why we were doing it a certain way and how we could do things even better and more efficiently.

Both Elyse and I continuously work to improve ourselves and each other, while not taking the world too seriously and having fun. As much as we're alike in so many ways, we're also different in some aspects. I guess that's what makes us a pretty good duo. Opposites attract, as they say.

What are your favourite memories with Elyse?
1. Completing *The Block* together and remaining a couple after it wrapped. The moment when we won the show was a pretty special moment for the two of us.

2. We had a gruelling 18 months of renovating our first home together. After all the hard work, the day we sold the house at the auction was a moment we'll never forget. Together we'd exceeded our expectations and shared an immense feeling of pride.

3. Our numerous travels and adventures are pretty high up on my list, too. We have seen some unbelievable places in our time together, and no doubt these adventures will continue for the rest of our lives.

Can you summarise Elyse in five words?
Most annoying person I love.

CHAPTER
TEN

Shaping
Your Future

The future of your life is in your hands. Of course things will pop up that we're unable to control, but for the most part, we need to celebrate that we live in a world bursting with opportunity. Step up, put your game face on and give life your all.

As each year passes, you'll become richer in both knowledge and experience. Don't doubt yourself; push yourself instead! Shape your future using excitement to fuel the fire in your belly. It's so easy to become overwhelmed as adult life becomes more serious, so take it day by day. Try your best and be accountable by choosing to actively make decisions about your future rather than just 'letting it happen' – from saving money to planning for big expenditures, buying real estate, travelling and so on. Life is what you make it, so make it fabulous!

Learning to save

I am a big believer in saving: putting your pennies away for something big. Aside from everyday expenditures (with a treat here and there), I aim to save as much as I can from each pay cheque. Why? Because there is no better time to start investing in your future than today! I don't mean to sound like your mum or dad, but there is so much truth to it. Clothes, shoes and nights out are short-term gains. Keep the long run in mind. Think about your savings in terms of the next two to five years instead of the next two to five weekends. Self control can be tough, I get it. However, I truly urge everyone to create a savings account and pop a little bit of money into it whenever you can.

When it comes to finances, my biggest advice is that good old-fashioned hard work is the best way to succeed. You might win the lottery or you may even inherit a bit of money, but that pure and genuine feeling of satisfaction will only come after you do the hard yards. Earning your own money and paying your own way is so, so liberating. Do your best to find a job that you adore. There is a perfect role out there for everyone, but it may take a bit of trial and error to find it. Patience and resilience are what you need to focus on.

I started working when I was in junior school. My earnings would go into an account that I didn't need to touch much as at that age there isn't all that much to buy. Dad would always remind me that leaving that money to grow over time was the smartest thing I could do. It could eventually enable me to use it for something big: a car, travel, a house (or even rent money and a bond if I wanted to move in with friends).

I told you at the beginning of the book that my first big buy was a Baby Born. Dad helped me count the notes and coins from my piggy bank and off we went to buy me a doll. I'll never forget the initial moment of sadness when I handed over my money. 'Goodbye sweet savings,' was all I could think. However, it took no time at all for an ear-to-ear smile to appear on my face. My baby was here! She was all mine. I cherished her even more because I'd earned her.

After my Baby Born came a slightly different kind of baby: a car! She was a tad more expensive, but the feeling of happiness and pride when I brought her home felt exactly the same. I'd saved

Do your best to find a job that you adore.

Committing to your savings and being sensible with your income means you can occasionally treat yourself to something special. I splurged on this bag recently ... I named her Avocado.

My handbag essentials

As I am on the run so often, my bag has become like a second home. I carry everything with me always!

Personal care

* Lip balm — I always carry at least two in case I misplace one. I actually go crazy if I don't have lip balm on me!

* Perfume oil — something small but with a strong scent.

* Eye drops — absolutely always!

* Tampons — no one likes to be surprised.

* Face wipes — taking my make-up off straight after work or before my flight home is a must

Essentials

* Keys
* Wallet

Health

* Panadol — for times when the music doesn't work fast enough.

* Protein bar

* Reusable water bottle

Calming

* Headphones — listening to music calms me down and encourages my mind to completely switch off. I depend on music at times because I tend to get shocker headaches if I let my brain keep ticking!

Fashion

* Sunglasses

* Strapless bra — I always carry a nude G for work purposes.

up for a long time and when I finally had enough money, I bought myself a little Honda CRV. It was black with a bright pink UNIT sticker on the back. I absolutely loved my new wheels. It had a camping table in the back, so I always had a wicked set-up when we went camping on the weekend. And having my own car meant that I could drive out of the city with my wakeboard or surfboard, find a bit of outback or coastal heaven and put the seats down to make a bed for overnight stays. What more could a girl want? This baby was bliss.

The bittersweet thing about these 'bigger' types of purchases is that they tend to come with associated or ongoing costs. (Happy days! #not) When you buy a car, you also have to pay for insurance, registration, petrol, parking and servicing. When you travel, you need to think about insurance and any required visas. And a house — you can only imagine how many joyful expenses come with buying a house! My point is, if you are going to commit to a 'big purchase', make sure you are ready for the 'big commitment' that follows.

Like many people, I am a big believer in the mindset of, 'You only live once!'. Experiencing life by going places and seeing things is all part of the ride. With this in mind, I approach 'spending' as a compromise. For example, if I want to eat out on the weekend, I'll pick one meal: dinner, lunch or brekkie. I get an experience, a yummy meal and a great outing, plus I save the rest. Simple.

Getting into property

Buying a house has always been a huge goal of mine. I think I inherited this from my parents. I saw how happy it made them to buy our family home and make it a special place for our family to grow up and create memories.

When I met Josh, I knew we were a good pairing. We're both strong-minded, determined and responsible people who share the goal of wanting to get ahead early in life. We work hard and we don't complain when times get a little tough. We both agreed it was a good time to get cracking on the property market and worked our butts off until we transformed our dream into a reality. I was only 21 when we purchased our first place in Coburg. It was daunting, let me assure you. But the excitement and pride trampled my fear pretty quickly.

We ended up buying the ugly duckling on the street — in the whole neighbourhood, actually! It was almost falling apart at the seams and the whole house was on a slant. Yep, it was totally lopsided. Josh could roll a coin from one side of the house to the other. It was a shack!

My parents were a little worried, to say the least, when they saw what we'd poured our hard-earned savings into. They looked a tad shocked but remained encouraging and supportive. We all knew that with Josh's skills, my patience (in other words, my ability to live in a dump) and our mutual ability to work hard and save, we'd be fine. There was so much potential with the old Coburg house. With time, renovations and all hands on deck, we were confident we could turn it into a masterpiece.

After a few years of showering outside with no walls, sleeping in one room out the back (in puffa jackets because it was that cold!), eating nothing but barbecues and raising a puppy (Isla), we did it. It took blood, sweat and tears, but the end result was spectacular. Josh and I sold the house at the end of 2017. We're delighted knowing the buyers now have a beautiful family home that will last the distance. We did a solid job!

Buying property isn't only about savings, of course. It's about taking a loan from the bank. This can be scary. Josh and I are similar in that we both like to step outside our comfort zone, knowing that with risk comes reward. There is really no way around borrowing a big chunk from the bank these days, so find comfort in the fact that most people have to do this. Having a mortgage is not a bad thing. Think of what you're getting in return: a house! An asset. Be proud of that.

Make sure you find a place and a loan amount that are comfortable for you. As long as you can comfortably make the repayments on the loan each week or month, you'll be fine. There's nothing to fear if you are organised.

Seeing the world

When it comes to big goals for savings, travel is also something I cherish and prioritise. Seeing the world is invaluable. Honestly, the places you will see, the cultures you can be immersed in and the people you'll meet will give you memories to last a lifetime. Travel shapes the person you are and the perspective you have. It opens your eyes to diversity. To travel is to explore the unknown. It's so special and something I hope you all strive towards.

I travel for fun, but also for work. It's important that I have, and maintain, a healthy network in various pockets around the world to create working opportunities. I have many clients in Sydney, for example, and Los Angeles. Making sure I travel to these cities is important as it shows my commitment to their markets. Travelling to the U.S. (mainly Los Angeles and New York City) is not cheap, so I always have to save up for a few months in advance. Flights, accommodation, insurance, living expenses — aah, it never ends! Being financially secure when you travel is a must.

I used to stay in model apartments when I was a teenager, but now I'm at a point in my life where space is essential. It was great to meet people and learn to live alongside other personalities, but as my career intensified, I needed a place to have a proper sleep with no interruptions. Elyse Knowles without sleep is scary! Thank god for Airbnb. I can now book a whole apartment in the inner city and save on things like Ubers and taxis because I'm able to walk from A to B.

Investing in yourself

When I'm in the States for work, it usually means long days — meeting clients and going to castings, fittings, shoots and test shoots. Test shoots are photo shoots that are planned purely to add to your portfolio. The difference between a test shoot and a paid shoot is that I pay for the test shoot. It's considered an investment, really.

If you have your own business, investing the money you earn back into your business is super important. You need to remain professional. For me, it's imperative to invest in test shoots at least a few times a year. They give me a chance to meet and work with

A very special moment shooting in Bora Bora.

Now this is pure happiness. I couldn't believe how clear the water was.

different creatives, play around with different looks (in terms of fashion, beauty, lighting, location, etc) and grow as a model. I do a lot of research before booking the team and spending my money to ensure I'll benefit from the new shots. After all, that's why you invest: to increase your earning potential.

A test shoot can cost a small fortune, let me tell you! By the time I pay for a photographer and their assistants, lighting, a stylist, hair and make-up, location, catering, travel and accommodation, it amounts to some big money. But don't let spending always scare you. While it seems like your money is vanishing quickly, focus on what you'll be receiving in return.

Giving back

After years of investing in property, travel and my business, I've been lucky to have experienced some gains. I don't mean to sound corny, but I am hugely grateful and humbled by where I am today. It's taken me a long time to get here (and I still have a long way to go and many goals to tick off), but I'm now at a point where giving back is high on my priority list. I've had beautiful opportunities in my life. It would mean the world to me to be able to create those same opportunities for other people in parts of the world where opportunities are slim to none.

One of my favourite types of travel is visiting new places to learn about their culture and how I can help to bring positive changes to certain communities. Between Josh and me, we have visited some beautiful places, such as all over Indonesia, Mexico, Jamaica, Lombok, Timor-Leste, Tahiti, Vanuatu, Bora Bora and Fiji. As soon as we get off the plane, we hire a scooter or a car and off we go. Our adventures always seem to end in a particular type of destination: somewhere we can find and spoil beautiful groups of vibrant kids! We try to map out little villages before we get going and we make it our aim to deliver toys, balls, cricket bats, stickers and colourful pencils. The smiles on the kids' faces is something you can't forget. These experiences make us feel incredibly fortunate to meet such beautiful and inspiring people.

It's easy to forget how lucky we are, particularly in Australia and New Zealand. We have healthy soil to grow food, a buzzing

Witnessing how your donations help people in need makes you want to cry. With very little of their own, these precious sweethearts gave me so much.

economy, amazing public transport, a strong education system and clean running water. We have so much goodness and so much potential at our fingertips. We live in an absolute paradise compared to many places around the world. Travelling in a variety of developing countries — learning about their struggles and misfortunes — has made me so much more aware of the world. I'm determined to give back as much as I can in my lifetime and I urge you to do the same.

One charity I've become involved with of late is WaterAid Australia. When I launched my label, Evrryday, I decided to donate profits to an amazing charity, and WaterAid was it. Since then, I've become more and more involved. Their efforts, time and commitment are spectacular.

WaterAid's goal is to get water, toilets and hygiene to the millions of people still living without them. It's hard to believe that turning a tap on to find dirty water — or no water at all — is a reality for many people. And what about not being about to flush the toilet? Or not being able to clean your house so that it's a hygienic environment for your kids? Imagine the hygiene of children who can barely bathe after a full day outside working. I recently travelled with the WaterAid Australia team to Timor-Leste to see the issue first-hand and gain a greater understanding of where the money raised was going. Let me assure you: it's going towards brilliant and essential things.

WaterAid Australia is on a mission to help developing countries such as Timor-Leste build hygienic and sustainable communities to improve their general living conditions, their economy and, most of all, their health. Watching the smiles on kids' faces when they saw water running from the tap was a shock. It looked as though they'd just met Santa Claus. They were in awe. These little kids and their families need support.

Without clean water, children are malnourished and have limited growth potential. For some of the mothers, finding water for their babies means hiking up huge hills, waiting for hours as their bucket fills up from the slowly trickling water, and then carrying it all the way back home — while balancing the weight of the water on their heads. Think about this the next time you open your water bottle and take a huge gulp. What a privilege that is. It was awful to witness such hardship, but I'm grateful I did, as I can now devote time to supporting the cause.

Charitable organisations are incredible. Do some research to find causes that are meaningful to you and within your reach, whether your goal is to contribute time or money. And never forget or take for granted what a charmed existence we lead.

The future is yours

To end this rather serious chapter, I just want to say: be brave and be responsible. Find a good accountant, ask questions when you are confused and don't rush into anything when you don't need to. Take your time to figure out what means the most to you in life. Where do you want to be in a few years' time? What's on your bucket list? Investing isn't about possessions and materialism; it's about building the foundations of your life: the floors you'll dance on, the skies you'll dance under. It's all in your hands.

Thank you

Things like this book don't happen easily; they take a big, collaborative team. I'm so thankful for my team for guiding me, never letting me down – and for agreeing to take me on to begin with!

The girl who has been by my side from day dot in my career is Tori Bowman. Tori, you continue to inspire me, guide me, motivate me and keep my life on track. You turn all of my ideas into realities. You hear my voice, you help me speak my thoughts and you make me stronger! You're the ultimate girl boss and a true friend who has had my back from the start. I've got yours too, gf! We've got this! Thank you.

My family, Josh and Isla, continue to push me to the limits and bring me back down to earth when it all gets too crazy. Without you guys, I'd be a crazy woman (even crazier than I am now). Thank you for believing in me and making my dreams come alive at every chance you get. The life we live together is very special to me and the love we share will never end.

Lots of love to my manager, Kate Heliotis. Together we make so many plans and set so many goals. I get worried we can't possibly do it all, but you have a way of making it all happen. It's like magic. We've only worked together for a short time but when you find a rock in this industry, you hold on for dear life. We'll keep going on this adventure together, side by side, watching each other grow. There's no stopping us.

To the brilliant people who took the time to share their wise words and advice in interviews: thank you. Each and every one of you fuel my ambition and perseverance. To have been able to include you in such a personal part of my career feels incredibly special. I am so grateful to have a collection of magnificent muses like you all!

Thank you to the special group of creatives who have watched me grow into the person I am today: Emily Abay, Lana Wilkinson, Brooke Meredith, Kate Fletcher, Monica Gingold, Lisa Frieling and Ed Purmono. You not only helped create the imagery for this book, but are helping me create a beautiful career. You are true friends and adored colleagues.

And last, but by no means least, thank you to everyone on the Murdoch Books team. From the original book scout, Claire Kingston, to Publisher Kelly Doust, Publishing Director Lou Johnson, Editorial Manager Julie Mazur Tribe, Creative Director Jacqui Porter and the team at Northwood Green, Editor Kay Halsey, Production Director Lou Playfair and Publicist Carol Warwick, thank you for thinking that my story is valuable. You taught me that my story could help others become the best versions of themselves — all with smiles on your faces! My story is now accessible to everyone in a book that's even more beautiful that I could have envisioned.

Thank you x

Published in 2018 by Murdoch Books, an imprint of Allen & Unwin
Reprinted in 2018

Murdoch Books Australia
83 Alexander Street
Crows Nest NSW 2065
Phone: +61 (0)2 8425 0100
murdochbooks.com.au
info@murdochbooks.com.au

For Corporate Orders & Custom Publishing, contact our Business Development Team at
salesenquiries@murdochbooks.com.au.

Publisher: Kelly Doust
Editorial Manager: Julie Mazur Tribe
Creative Direction: northwoodgreen.com
Editor: Kay Delves
Photographer: Emily Abay, unless otherwise specified
Production Director: Lou Playfair

For all images except those noted below, thank you to the creative team of Lana Wilkinson, Kate Fletcher,
Monica Gingold and Lisa Frieling (video)

Credits:
Page 48: photography by David Gubert, courtesy of Megan Gale. © David Gubert.
Page 82: photography by Hannah Scott-Stevenson at Artboxblack for Seafolly. © Seafolly.
Page 83: photography by Toby Peet for Seafolly. © Seafolly.
Pages 84, 96–98, 101, 141 (denim jacket, Converse shoes), 142, 146, 147, 203: photography by Brooke Meredith.
© Brooke Meredith.
Page 86: photography by Mike McLaughlin. © Mike McLaughlin.
Pages 108–109: photography by Tom Ross for Vital-All-In-One. © Vital-All-In-One.
Page 116: photography by David Higgs for A Conscious Collection. © A Conscious Collection.
Page 141 (Elyse on bicycle, Elyse in sunglasses): photography by Chris Bagot. © Chris Bagot.
Pages 142, 170, 171: photography by Ed Purnomo. © Ed Purnomo.
Page 166: Stellar cover photography by Tane Coffin.

A cataloguing-in-publication entry is available from the catalogue of the National Library of Australia at nla.gov.au.

ISBN 978 1 76052 396 1 Australia

Colour reproduction by Splitting Image Colour Studio Pty Ltd, Clayton, Victoria
Printed by WKT Company Limit, China